PRAISE FOR NAPOLEON HILL
FROM GREAT MINDS AND LEADERS

The 12 Miracles of Life has lain dormant for 75 or more years before this definitive edition came to be published. It is Napoleon Hill's "newest" book, based on his famous Law of Success philosophy. His work and writings have been praised by great leaders in finance, education, scientific invention, government, and political life, including:

Supreme Court of the United States, Washington, D.C.

"My Dear Mr. Hill: I have now had an opportunity to finish reading your Law of Success textbooks, and I wish to express my appreciation of the splendid work you have done in the philosophy. It would be helpful if every politician in the country could assimilate and apply the principles upon which the Law of Success is based. It contains some very fine material which every leader in every walk of life should understand."

 —William H. Taft, tenth Chief Justice and twenty-seventh
  President of the United States of America and Chief
  Justice

Laboratory of Thomas A. Edison

"My Dear Mr. Hill: Allow me to express my appreciation of the compliment you have paid me in sending me the original manuscript of *Law of Success*. I can see you have spent a great deal of time and thought in its preparation. Your philosophy is sound and you are to be congratulated for sticking to your work over so long a period of years. Your students . . . will be amply rewarded for their labor."

—Thomas A. Edison, inventor and entrepreneur

"The principles . . . are both practical and sound. I was one of Mr. Hill's first students, long before his philosophy gained world-wide fame. Whatever success I may have attained I owe to the principles covered by this philosophy, some of which I applied unconsciously. I am proud to know that an intimate personal friend of mine has had the honor of producing the world's first practical philosophy of financial success."

—Edwin C. Barnes, salesman and business associate of
    Thomas A. Edison

Public Ledger, Philadelphia

"Dear Mr. Hill, Thank you for your *Law of Success*. It is great stuff."

—Cyrus H. K. Curtis, publisher of *Saturday Evening Post*
    and *Ladies Home Journal*

"The best evidence of the soundness of the Law of Success, with which I am personally acquainted is the noteworthy achieve-ment of Mr. Curtis, who has built one of the greatest publish-ing businesses in the world by applying the principles of this philosophy."

—Edward Bok, editor *Ladies Home Journal* and Pulitzer-
    prize-winning author of *The Americanization of
    Edward Bok*

King of the 5 and 10 Cent Stores

"By applying many of the fundamentals of the *Law of Success* philosophy, we have built a great chain of successful stores. I presume it would be no exaggerations of fact if I said that the Woolworth Building might properly be called a monument to the soundness of these principles."

—F. W. Woolworth, entrepreneur and founder of
    F. W. Woolworth Company

Great Steamship Magnate

"I feel greatly indebted for the privilege of reading your *Law of Success*. If I had had this philosophy fifty years ago, I suppose I should have accomplished all that I have done in less than half the time. I sincerely hope the world will discover and reward you."

—Captain Robert Dollar, industrialist known as the
    "Grand Old Man of the Pacific" and founder of Dollar
    Steamship Lines

Great Scientist and Inventor

"Answering your inquiry concerning the work of Napoleon Hill, I am happy to tell you that I gave him free access to my entire life's labor of research, on the subject of vibration, for use in his *Law of Success* philosophy. He has, in my opinion, produced commendable philosophy which will live long after he shall have passed on."

—Alexander Graham Bell, scientist, engineer, and inventor
    of the telephone

Historic Labor Leader

"Mastery of the *Law of Success* philosophy is the equivalent of an insurance policy against failure."

> —Samuel Gompers, founder of the American Federation of Labor

Architect of the League of Nations and a Former President of the United States of America

"May I congratulate you on your persistence. Any man who devotes that much time . . . must of necessity make discoveries of great value to others. I am deeply impressed by your interpretation of the "Master Mind" principles which you have so clearly described."

> —Woodrow Wilson, academic, president of Princeton University, thirty-fourth governor of New Jersey, and twenty-eighth president of the United States of America

Merchant Prince and Department Store Founder

"I know that your seventeen fundamentals of success are sound because I have been applying them in my business for more than 30 years."

> —John Wanamaker, merchant and founder of Wanamaker's

World's Largest Maker of Cameras and Film

"I know that you are doing a world of good with your *Law of Success*. I would not care to set a monetary value on this training because it brings to the student qualities which cannot be measured by money alone."

> —George Eastman, entrepreneur and founder of Eastman Kodak Company

Pioneer in Agricultural Science

"Your work and mine are peculiarly alike. I am helping the laws of Nature to create more perfect specimens of vegetations while you are using those same laws, through the *Law of Success*, to build more perfect specimens of thinkers."

 —Luther Burbank, botanist and horticulturist

Internationally Known Food and Candy Business Chief

"Whatever success I may have attained I owe entirely to the application of your principles of the *Law of Success*. I believe I have the honor of being your first student."

 —William Wrigley, Jr., industrialist and founder of
  Wm. Wrigley Jr. Company

Hotel Chain Founder

"Our entire business policy, in the management of our hotels, is based upon the . . . fundamentals of the *Law of Success*, of which I am a student."

 —E. M. Statler, businessman and founder of Statler Hotels

Renowned Educator and University President

"Napoleon Hill has produced what I believe to be the first practical philosophy of achievement. Its major distinguishing feature is the simplicity in which it has been presented."

 —David Starr Jordan, ichthyologist, professor of zoology,
  and founding president of Stanford University

Rough Rider and a Former President of the United States of America

"Certainly I will supply you with the information you request. This I consider to be not only a duty, but it is a pleasure as well. You are laboring in behalf of the people who have neither the time nor the inclination to ferret out the causes of failure and success."

—Theodore "Teddy" Roosevelt, politician, soldier, conservationist, historian, naturalist, explorer, writer, thirty-third governor of New York, twenty-fifth vice president, and twenty-sixth president of the United States of America

One of the Richest People in Modern History

"You may say for Mr. Rockefeller that he endorses Mr. Hill's seventeen fundamental principles of success, and that he recommends them to those who are seeking the highway to achievement."

—John D. Rockefeller, business magnate, philanthropist, and founder of Standard Oil Company

THE 12 MIRACLES OF LIFE

THE **12** MIRACLES OF LIFE

THE SCIENCE OF SUCCESS

NAPOLEON HILL

Humanix Books
www.humanixbooks.com

Humanix Books
The 12 Miracles of Life
Copyright © 2025 by Napoleon Hill Foundation
All rights reserved.

Humanix Books, P.O. Box 20989, West Palm Beach, FL 33416, USA
www.humanixbooks.com | info@humanixbooks.com

Humanix Books is a division of Humanix Publishing, LLC. Its trademark, consisting of the words "Humanix Books," is registered in the United States Patent and Trademark Office and in other countries.

Humanix Books titles may be purchased for educational, business, or sales promotional use. For information about special discounts for bulk purchases, please contact the Special Markets Department at info@humanixbooks.com.

ISBN: 978-1-63006-286-6 (Hardcover)
ISBN: 978-1-63006-287-3 (E-book)

Printed in the United States of America
10 9 8 7 6 5 4 3 2 1

ABOUT LIFE

Life, you can't subdue me because I refuse to take your discipline too seriously. When you try to hurt me, I laugh—and the laughter knows no pain. I appreciate your joys wherever I find them; your sorrows neither frighten nor discourage me, for there is laughter in my soul.

Temporary defeat does not make me sad. I simply set music to the words of defeat and turn it into a song. Your tears are not for me, for I like laughter much better, and because I like it, I use it as a substitute for grief and sorrow and pain and disappointment.

Life, you are a fickle trickster—don't deny it. You slipped the emotion of love into my heart so that you might use it as a thorn with which to prick my soul—but I learned to dodge your trap with laughter. You tried to lure me with the desire for gold, but I have fooled you by following the trail which leads to knowledge instead. You induced me to build beautiful friendships—then converted my friends to enemies so you may harden my heart, but I sidestepped your figure on this by laughing off your attempts and selecting new friends in my own way.

You caused men to cheat me at trade so I will become distrustful, but I won again because I possess one precious asset which no man can steal—it is the power to think my own thoughts and to be myself. You threaten me with death, but to me death is nothing worse than a long peaceful sleep, and sleep is the sweetest of human experiences—excepting laughter.

You build a fire of hope in my heart, then sprinkle water on the flames, but I can go you one better by rekindling the fire—and I laugh at you once more.

You have nothing that can lure me away from laughter, and you are powerless to scare me into submission. To a life of laughter, then, I raise my cup of cheer!

Napoleon Hill

Contents

Foreword

Napoleon Hill, pioneer in the study of the American philosophy of personal achievement, was born on October 26, 1883, in Wise County, Virginia, a region in the Blue Ridge Mountains where literacy and superstition were widespread. His father was a blacksmith, and the family lived in a one-room, dirt-floor cabin, common in the region.

Young Napoleon Hill (named for a rich uncle) was an unruly, aggressive child. When he was nine, his mother died, leaving him with his father who had difficulty disciplining the boy. Napoleon enjoyed playing pranks on neighbors. As he grew more daring, he carried a six-shooter (he idolized the outlaw Jesse James). He was the toughest boy in the county and proud of it.

Fortunately, his stepmother took him aside, and calmly and compassionately said something to the boy that would cause a dramatic reversal in him. "She called me into the living room in private," Hill later recalled:

> *. . . and not only changed the course of my life, but also planted in my mind a desire to become self-determining*

by rendering useful service. . . . She said that people
misjudged me—I was not the worst boy in the county, only
the most active, and I needed a definite purpose to which
I could direct my attentions. She told me that I had a keen
imagination and plenty of initiative. She suggested that I
become a writer, saying that if I would devote as much time
to reading and writing as I had been to causing trouble in the
neighborhood, I might live to see the time when my influence
would be felt throughout the state.

The following year, at fifteen, Hill completed grade school
and began to work part time as a newspaper reporter, writing
local items for a dozen small town papers, throughout Virginia.
Looking back, he admitted that his writing wasn't "brilliant," but
that it was "readable because it was written with so much enthusiasm." After completing his school, Hill enrolled in a one-year
course at a nearby business college.

At eighteen, fascinated by legal work, Hill felt he would make
law a career and hoped to enter Georgetown University Law
School. But there was an obstacle: he had no money to finance his
education. To earn his tuition, he decided to return to journal-
ism and specialize in biographical stories about successful people,
something several magazines of the period were publishing.

His first step was to approach former Tennessee Governor
Robert L. Taylor, publisher of *Bob Taylor's Magazine*. It didn't
take long for Taylor to recognize potential in Hill; he hired him
halfway through their meeting. Taylor offered to compose let-
ters of introduction for Hill to prominent individuals who might
make good subjects for profiles, and he tossed out names for Hill's
consideration: Thomas Edison, John Wanamaker, publishers

Edward Bok and Cyrus H. K. Curtis, Alexander Graham Bell, and Andrew Carnegie. Dazzled by these prospects, Hill decided to give up his plans to study law and spend all his time writing.

In the fall of 1908, as Hill described it, "The Hand of Destiny reached out." He was on his way to Pittsburgh. Andrew Carnegie had granted him an interview. Hill went directly to Carnegie's office and drove into the questioning: "Mr. Carnegie, to what do you attribute your phenomenal success?" The industrialist, then seventy-three, opened up quickly and with wit and his unrivaled gift for anecdote, began to relate the story of his achievements.

Hill could hardly keep up his shorthand notes when Carnegie then began to expound on his own and others' theories of personal achievement. Then Carnegie lamented. "It's a shame that each new generation must find the way to success by trial and error when the principles really are clear-cut." He suggested to Hill that the world needed a practical philosophy of individual achievement that would help the humblest worker to accumulate riches in whatever amount and form he might desire.

After a three-hour session, to Hill's astonishment, Carnegie invited him back for three days, Carnegie elaborated on his idea, describing how one might go about the organization of such a philosophy.

"You now have my idea of a new philosophy," Carnegie said, "and I wish to ask you a question in connection with it, which I want you to answer by a simple 'yes' or 'no.'"

"If I give you the opportunity to organize the world's first philosophy of individual achievement, and introduce you to men who can and will collaborate with you in its organization, do you want the opportunity, and will you follow through with it if it is given to you?"

Hill stammered for a few seconds, and then blurted out with characteristic enthusiasm, "Yes! I'll undertake the job—and I'll finish it."

Carnegie drew out a stopwatch and told Hill that it had taken him exactly twenty-nine seconds to respond to the question, and he had been giving him a maximum of sixty seconds to reach his decision. If he had gone over that time, the opportunity would have been withdrawn: "It has been my experience that a man who cannot reach a decision promptly cannot be depended upon to carry through any decision he may make. I have also discovered that men who reach decisions promptly usually have the capacity to move with definiteness of purpose in other circumstances.

"Very well. You have one of the two important qualities that will be needed by the man who organizes the philosophy I have described. Now I will learn whether or not you have the second.

"If I give you this opportunity, are you willing to devote twenty years of your time to research the causes of success and failure without pay, earning your own living as you go along?"

Hill was stunned. He had assumed that Carnegie would subsidize him from his enormous fortune.

"It is not unwillingness to supply the money," Carnegie explained. "It is my desire to know if you have in you the natural capacity to *go the extra mile*—that is, to render service before trying to collect for it."

Napoleon Hill met Carnegie's second test. He would go on to write the American philosophy of personal achievement. He would also become an esteemed lecturer, educator, and confidential advisor to two presidents, as well as prolific author on the subject of personal achievement.

Throughout Hill's years of research, Carnegie remained steadfast. He did not reimburse Hill for his efforts, compelling the young man to work to support himself and later a family. As a result, Hill's professional life took many turns.

When the United States entered World War I, President Woodrow Wilson (who, when he was head of Princeton University, had met Hill through Andrew Carnegie) asked Hill to come to the White House to serve as his public-relations advisor. Hill jumped at the opportunity. He was at Wilson's side in 1918 when a dispatch announced that the Germans were requesting armistice, and he helped the president formulate his reply.

With the election of a new administration, Hill left Washington and spent a brief stint editing and publishing *Golden Rule* magazine. But his thoughts began to turn back to the field of education and after a year, he left *Golden Rule* to spend his time teaching and lecturing. Soon he became a widely acclaimed and much-sought-after speaker.

He always spoke on the Law of Success, spreading the ideas and philosophy that he was gleaning from his study of the factors that produced success and failure. In 1923, Hill began to transcribe his voluminous notes to manuscript form, and in 1928 the sixteen-lesson course, *Law of Success*, was finally in print. It has taken Hill twenty years to complete this project, exactly as Carnegie had predicted. With the publication of *Law of Success*, Hill's star skyrocketed. His royalties hit $2,500 per month and stayed there for years. The book was eventually distributed worldwide.

Hill described his work as a "blueprint that may be followed straight to success" and claimed he was simply, "organizing old truths and known laws into practical, usable form, where they may be properly interpreted and applied by the workaday man whose needs call for a philosophy of simplicity."

"My purpose was twofold," Hill said:

First, to help the earnest student find out what his or her weaknesses are. Second, to help create a definite plan for bridging those weaknesses. The most successful men and women on earth have had to correct certain weak spots in their personalities before they began to succeed.

You cannot enjoy outstanding success in life without power, and you can never enjoy power without sufficient personality to influence other people to cooperate with you in a spirit of harmony. This course shows you, step by step, how to develop such a personality. The student who takes up this course with an open mind, and sees to it that his or her mind remains open until the last lesson has been read, will be richly rewarded with a broader and more accurate view of life as a whole.

Hill served President Franklin D. Roosevelt as an advisor throughout most of the Depression years. He said that as a presidential speech writer, he wrote much of the contents of the famous Fireside Chats and he conceived the theme, "We have nothing to fear but fear itself."

Don M. Green
Executive Director of the Napoleon Hill Foundation

Note on the Text from the Napoleon Hill Foundation

THE UNIQUENESS OF NAPOLEON HILL'S "MIRACLES OF LIFE" MANUSCRIPT

Having given you the background on the significance of Napoleon Hill the person, as well as his prolific publishing history, here's a few insights on the never-before-published manuscript that you are about to read. While this manuscript is known to be written by Napoleon Hill himself (and actually had his own handwritten changes penciled into the text), the exact timing and reason for this publication is unknown. We know it was never published. We know it contains material we have never seen before in any of his works. We know from events in the manuscript that it was written sometime between 1949 and 1965, and portions of it suggest it was written late in this period. We know it is incomplete. And given that the original chapters were somewhat jumbled, we did some of our own editing to make this text an enjoyable and memorable reading experience. Hill wrote that it contained chapters devoted to twelve miracles, and it does, but one can tell from reading it that 13 miracles were originally to be discussed, including one "major" miracle. The last chapter appears to be missing. And the chapter titled "How to Transmute the Creative Force of Sex," reads as if it may have been intended for another book.

We have done only very minor editing to the manuscript, finding it interesting to see some of Hill's changes. It is interesting in many other ways. It does not discuss each of the seventeen principles of Hill's *The Science of Personal Achievement*. It contains chapters devoted to concepts Hill did not include in those principles, such as "The Mastery of Poverty," "Sorrow as the Path to the Soul," and "Wisdom Robs Death of its Sting." In one chapter Hill offers to sell the reader a phonograph that will teach a foreign language "while you sleep." In another, he lists fifty-four causes of failure. He has some very unkind things to say about his father, but then says his father changed his ways for the better due to the intervention of his second wife.

We at the Napoleon Hill Foundation are still finding unpublished material by Napoleon Hill in our archives. He was a prolific writer. Maybe we will find more clues to when and why this manuscript was written and whether there is a missing chapter. If so, we will publish those as later editions of this manuscript. Meanwhile, it is our intention to bring these timeless thoughts and insights of this inspirational thinker to you, as close as possible to their original form. We hope you find the reading experience to be enjoyable—and most important, life-changing!

Preface

A VISIT THROUGH THE VALLEY
OF LIFE'S MIRACLES

A little while ago I turned back the pages of the Great Book of Time in which my own magnificent interlude with Life has been recorded, and on the pages marked "Things I Have Discarded as Being Either Harmless or Useless in Life," I discovered a gold mine of riches which I shall reveal through this volume.

Why did I wait so long to make this discovery of the fabulous riches I had overlooked?

The answer will be obvious when the nature of my discovery has been described. Before I could make this discovery, I had to become of age spiritually; I had to trade youth for maturity of age in order to gain sufficient wisdom, to give me the capacity to recognize and properly interpret these great riches from within, through eyes which are not deceived by the false habits of men.

As I slowly turned the pages of this astounding record in the Great Book of Time, I was shocked to discover that everything, every circumstance known to man, every mistake, every failure, and every heartache, may become highly beneficial when one relates to them in a spirit of harmony and understanding of their nature and purpose.

And I was agreeably surprised to learn, by analyzing all the circumstances of my past which I had considered unpleasant and harmful at the time, *that each of these yielded the things of permanent value which I now possess.*

During my exploration of this Great Book of Time, I discovered a previously unknown method by which all of man's past failures and mistakes and frustrations may be transmuted into the richest blessings known to mankind. It was this discovery which left me no alternative but to write this volume, for the benefit of those who are groping in darkness for the way to peace of mind, just as I was blindly searching for it for nearly forty years.

Before I rummaged through the scrapheap of the ideas and things I discarded as useless, I believed the secret of successful achievement could be revealed only by studying those who were successful.

Having been commissioned by Andrew Carnegie to give the world its first practical philosophy of success, and through Mr. Carnegie having had close access to more than five hundred of the top-ranking successes of his era, I naturally looked to these men of great achievement as the only source of usable knowledge worthy of consideration by those who are trying to find their places in an intensively competitive world. This false conclusion I have now abandoned, for I have discovered that the eternal laws of successful human achievement are as available to the poor and the humble as they are to the rich and the proud.

My first shocking realization of this great truth came with my first meeting with an uneducated little man who was born in the South and earned his bread by the sweat of his brow. When I first heard of his story, I sought him out and gave him a searching and critical analysis, for I had a keen desire to learn the true secret of his dramatic rebirth from rags to riches within an unbelievable brief time.

On a hot summer day this man stopped at the end of a row of cotton, leaned on his hoe-handle, mopped his brow and cried out in agony:

> *Oh Lord! Why do I have to work like this and get nothing out of it but a hut to sleep in and sow-belly to eat?*

His cry brought an answer the likes of which no other man had ever heard and started a series of circumstances which have changed millions of the lives of people who were destined to hear his story.

I have chosen this humble man's story as an introduction to this chapter because it so perfectly illustrates the soundness of the counsel I shall offer through subsequent chapters, to those who are searching for material riches, peace of mind, and a better understanding of the means of mastering all unpleasant circumstances.

Because of the place of his birth and poverty, this man had two strikes against him from the start, *but purely by that chance question* he tuned in on one of the great miracles of life which will be described later, and lifted himself to a position of fame and fortune unknown to the majority of peoples, even those who have had the privilege of formal educations in our great universities.

First of all, the answer to the man's question gave him contact with the first principle of personal success, *Definiteness of Purpose*, and a definite plan for its attainment. And that purpose was nothing less than the trading of his old personality for a much greater one—a personality *with the power to get whatever he desired regardless of race, creed, or color*: the sort of personality I shall endeavor to help every reader of this volume to attain.

Forthwith, in compliance with the answer the man received to his question, he appointed himself to the high Priesthood as God in Person, the one and only true living God to all the people on earth. Whatever one may think of the man's choice of a Definite Major Purpose, he cannot be charged with an inferiority complex.

Now, before any conclusions are reached concerning this man's self-appointment to so high a station in life, let me give a briefing as to how far he has already gone in the attainment of his Definite Major Purpose. Perhaps you will sober your judgment of him, and instead of condemning him it just might be more beneficial if you found out something of the powers he adopted to raise himself to the high station in life he has thus far attained.

The man gave himself the very impressive pseudonym of "Father Divine" (see the Appendix), and at the time of this writing it has been said that he claims to have a following of *over thirty million people*, located in practically every state in the country and in some foreign countries. As to the correctness of this claim, there seems to be no practical way to determine it, but there is very definite proof that these followers have, regardless of their number, made Father Divine one of the richest men in the nation.

His money comes to him through voluntary gifts, often from unknown donators, and it is free from government taxation. When the Father desires to purchase an additional estate, or anything else he chooses, he pays in cash, of which he seems to possess an inexhaustible supply.

He travels in a chauffeur-driven Rolls-Royce automobile, and he sleeps in his own hotels in many of the cities he visits, so there never is any question of his getting hotel accommodations. And he operates businesses in a great variety of lines, all the way from push carts to dress shops and restaurants, with help that never goes on strikes or demands higher pay, because most of it is voluntary help.

How much good or evil this man's opulence may bring to himself or others is of no concern here, and to make sure that you get the full dramatic meaning of the story as it fits into the mosaic of this volume, be assured that the author is neither one of Father Divine's followers, nor is it his purpose to sell the Father to his readers.

However, it is the author's purpose to acquaint you with the nature of the "miracle" this man stumbled upon, perhaps by sheer chance, which gave him freedom from the handicap of his poverty and lack of education and made him fabulously rich through a source of *riches which cannot be stolen from him by any means known to man.*

This information is intended for your benefit, not that you may emulate Father Divine, but to inspire you to excel him in your own chosen field of service to mankind, whether it be in the realm of religion or in some other useful service. Or you may be content to use the information merely for softening the burdens of your own personal life.

The secret of Father Divine's riches is not new to me. I have devoted over forty years to its study, and I have seen it work successfully in the lives of more than five hundred of the top-ranking men of this nation with whom I worked, and who collaborated with me over a long period of years in the organization of the Science of Success—men like Henry Ford, Thomas A. Edison, Dr. Alexander Graham Bell, Woodrow Wilson, and William Howard Taft.

And the strangest fact concerning this supreme secret of personal success, as revealed by close study of those distinguished men with whom I worked, was that not one of them, with the exception of three, understood the real source of their success or the nature of the power which made it possible on so fabulous a scale. The vast majority of them stumbled upon this great "miracle" very much in the same manner as did the little cotton field man *who now rates as the richest clergyman in this or any other country.*

He has not only demonstrated his power to acquire and hold material riches in whatever amounts he desires, but also the ability to fully protect himself against his jealous enemies, whose main complaint against him probably is that they do not know the secret of his financial success. In this respect, an uneducated man has accomplished, single-handed and without outside help, that which 95 percent of the people of the world never accomplish during an entire lifetime. *He has acquired financial independence far beyond his needs.*

Some may question the man's concentration upon material wealth and point to this as evidence of his neglect of the spiritual qualities in which most clergymen specialize. But those who are seeking the true secret of his achievements will not overlook the fact that if he has a voluntary following of thirty million people, or even one million, he must possess some mysterious power of attraction not usually possessed by those who are motivated entirely by greed for material things. Here, as in other chapters, the author has endeavored to emphasize the fact that the secret of financial prosperity is precisely the same as that through which one may transmute physical pain or any unpleasant circumstance into benefits.

In this chapter, and in those which follow, I shall fully describe the "miracle" responsible for Father Divine's success, but I shall do more than that: I shall describe some additional miracles available to all the people of the earth, miracles which are only partially recognized and seldom used, although they provide the real path to peace of mind and material riches in abundance.

All, except approximately one person out of every ten million people who may read the list of miracles I shall here describe, will be shocked and surprised to learn that I have listed them as potential riches of the highest order. That one person out of every ten million will not be shocked or surprised because he or she will belong in the same class with the Edisons and the Fords and the Father Divines who stumbled upon the miracle and is using it to shape his destiny to his own self-styled pattern of life.

As we travel through the Valley of Life's Miracles," one of which was definitely responsible for Father Divine's transition from extreme poverty and ignorance into fabulous wealth and wisdom sufficient to manage it, you will have reason to rejoice if you recognize the particular miracle by which this change was wrought. If you do not make the discovery in this chapter, it may be revealed to you in subsequent chapters, where I have recorded all that is known of the path that leads to peace of mind and plenty.

Here are some cues which may aid you in analyzing Father Divine accurately:

The exact time, place, and circumstances where his new birth took place were matters entirely of his own choice *and under his control.*

No one aided him or suggested to him the possibility of his throwing off ignorance and poverty, and taking on, in their place, fabulous wealth and wisdom far beyond that of the majority of people. This point is emphasized because naturally it suggests that *whatever an uneducated man has done, any other person of equal mental capacity may duplicate or excel,* in any chosen field of human endeavor.

Our nation has produced many distinguished members of the human race, among them Booker T. Washington and Dr. George Washington Carver, but the little cotton field man who elected himself as God has projected himself into more space and attracted a greater following than all of the other members of his own race combined. At the same time, he has made himself one of the richest men who ever lived, and he has established a perpetual source of riches which will never diminish as long as he lives.

Could anyone reasonably doubt that the formula through which this man exchanged poverty for vast riches may also serve to transmute any undesirable circumstance into a benefit of equivalent proportions?

Father Divine's money-accumulating abilities have been emphasized, not because of any virtues which may be attached to those who possess money in great quantities, but for the reason that the majority of the people find it exceedingly difficult to secure enough to keep soul and body together during their lives.

Therein does the difference exist between this particular man and the others who live in the United States, and who have the same privileges he has acquired for himself? The answer to this question may give you a sound cue to the miracle which transformed this self-appointed Messiah, from a nobody, in the direst of poverty, to a somebody in command of overabundance.

The miracle responsible for Father Divine's changed life is precisely the same as that which lifted Henry Ford, Thomas A. Edison, and Andrew Carnegie to stupendous heights of personal achievement in their respective fields, and it is the same miracle which has been responsible for all the progress made by the human race in all fields of endeavor.

Through the aid of this miracle Mahatma Gandhi forced the once powerful British Empire to give India her freedom, and this despite the fact that Gandhi had no armies or military forces, no financial means, no house in which to live, and not even a pair of pants.

With the aid of the same miracle Milo C. Jones, owner of a small farm near Fort Atkinson, Wisconsin, made himself a millionaire after he had been stricken with double paralysis; and he found his incredible financial success on the same small farm where he lived.

Students of the author who have found prosperity, solved impossible personal problems, and found peace of mind through the aid of the miracle are legion. They exist in nearly every walk of life, every business, every profession, throughout a large portion of the world. For this reason, the illustrations given throughout this volume have been adequately authenticated over more than forty years of research.

Dr. Frank Crane was the pastor of a small church in Chicago, from which he barely earned a living. As a student of this author, he discovered the miracle that yielded him the idea of publishing his sermons in a syndicated newspaper column which brought him an income of more than $75,000 yearly.

What has all this to do with the mastery of fear and physical pain and sorrow, and the multiple frustrations one may encounter throughout life? Just how can the principle which helps people to become financially rich serve as well to separate physical pain from the dentist's drill or the surgeon's scalpel?

Be patient, read carefully with an open mind, and you shall have the answers to these and all other questions which may arise in your mind before the miracle is revealed to you.

If you should impatiently demand that the miracle be revealed in the first chapter of this volume, the author would answer by telling you the story of something which happened while he was a very small boy, but which made a lasting impression on his mind: Grandfather took some corn out to the chicken house, scattered it around over the dirt floor, and then carefully covered it with straw. When asked why he went to all this trouble, he replied, "For two very good reasons: number one, covering the corn with straw so the chicken will have to scratch to find it gives them exercise they need to be healthy, and secondly, it gives them a chance to get pleasure from showing how smart they are in finding the corn which they think I tried to hide from them."

And now let us turn to the analysis of some of the minor miracles one must understand and properly evaluate before the nature of the major miracle, which gives one a transformed life, can be revealed. Perhaps the most misunderstood of all these miracles is the one described in the next chapter because it reveals the starting place from which one must take off in exchanging the circumstances of life he does not desire for those which he covets.

THE 12
MIRACLES
OF LIFE

"You can do it if you think you can."

—*Success Through a Positive Mental Attitude*

The First Miracle of Life

THE INEXORABLE POWER OF FAITH

FAITH, the greatest of all known powers available to man, is a state of mind—a positive state of mind directed to definite ends.

An expectant father was pacing up and down the hall in front of the operating room at the hospital, waiting to hear whether it was a boy or a girl.

The door opened, two nurses came out and passed by the waiting father without looking in his direction. Then the doctor came to the door, hesitated a moment and motioned to the waiting father to come in.

"Before you go in" the doctor began, "I must prepare you for a shock! It's a boy and he was born without ears. He hasn't the slightest sign of ears, and of course he will be deaf and dumb all his life."

"He may have been born without ears" the father exclaimed, "but he will not go through life deaf and dumb!"

"Now don't become excited" said the doctor, "but you may as well prepare yourself to accept the conditions as they are; not as you wish them to be. Medical science has known of other cases like that of your son, but not one of the children born in his condition ever learned to hear or speak."

"Doctor, I have great respect for your skill as a physician, but I am also a doctor in a certain sense, for I have discovered a powerful remedy sufficient for human needs in practically every circumstance. The first step one must take in applying this remedy is to refuse to accept, as inevitable, any circumstance one does not desire, *and I am notifying you here and now that I shall never accept my son's affliction as something which cannot be corrected.*"

The doctor made no reply, but the look of astonishment on his face clearly said, "You poor fellow, I feel sorry for you, but you'll find out there are some circumstances of life which one is forced to accept." He took the father by the arm and walked into the room where the mother and child awaited him, pulled back the cover and stood silently while the father looked at what the doctor sincerely believed to be one of those "circumstances of life which one is forced to accept."

Time moved onward rapidly. Twenty-five years later another doctor smilingly emerged from his laboratory with some X-rays in his hands. "Miraculous," he exclaimed, "I have x-rayed this young man's head from every possible angle, and I see no evidence that he possesses any form of hearing equipment. Yet my tests show that he has 65 percent of his normal hearing capacity."

The doctor was Irving Voorhees, a well-known ear specialist in New York City, and the X-rays he held in his hands were made from the head of the young man who doubtlessly would have gone through life deaf and dumb had it not been for the intervention of a father who refused to accept that condition and did something to cause Nature to correct it.

I can vouch for the correctness of these statements because I am the father who refused to accept, as incurable, even so great an affliction as that of being born without ears.

For almost nine years I devoted a major portion of my time to the application of a power which finally restored to my son 65 percent of his normal hearing. It was sufficient to enable him to go through the graded school, high school, and college with grades that equaled the best of students. And it was sufficient to enable him to adjust himself to life so as to live normally and without inconveniences or embarrassment such as most deaf and dumb persons suffer.

How was this "miracle" performed?

Who or what did the performing, and what took place inside of the head of the child born without ears which enabled him to develop sufficient hearing capacity to carry him through life satisfactorily?

These same questions were put to Dr. Irving Voorhees. Here is his reply: "Without doubt the psychological directives the father gave through the child's subconscious mind influenced Nature to improvise some sort of a nerve system which connected the brain with the inner walls of the skull, thus enabling him to hear by what is now known as a bone conduction."

It is hoped that by the time you will have finished reading this volume, the exact nature of the "miracle" which saved a child from going through life as a deaf and dumb person will be revealed.

The author has been aided by this "miracle" ever since he first became conscious of it, when he was quite a young man. It has helped him to master fear, superstition, ignorance, and poverty, the four enemies of mankind to which so many people yield without a fight because they do not understand how to apply the miracle in refusing to accept from life that which *they do not want.*

The exact nature of the miracle is something one person cannot describe to another until that person has been mentally conditioned to receive it. For this *reason* it may be necessary for the reader to read and analyze all the subsequent chapters of this book before being conditioned to receive the full meaning of the miracle.

Some very definite clues have been described in this chapter, but they may not be sufficient to reveal the supreme secret by which one may successfully reject from life that which one does not desire. This secret is worth searching because it is the master key that will unlock the doors to multiple blessings for all who possess it, including the mastery of dread of dental and medical surgery.

The mental attitude in which you read this book will determine, to a large extent, the time and the place in the book where the secret may be revealed to you. Therefore, let us turn our attention to some of the profound potentials of a POSITIVE MENTAL ATTITUDE.

YOUR MENTAL ATTITUDE: THE ONLY THING YOU CONTROL OUTRIGHT

Get your mental attitude under control, and you may control almost all other circumstances which affect your life, including your fears and your worries of every nature whatsoever.

How Important Is Mental Attitude?

Let us analyze the part mental attitude plays in our lives, and we shall learn how important it is.

Your mental attitude is the major factor which attracts people to you in a spirit of friendliness or repels them, according to whether your attitude is positive or negative, and you are the only person who can determine which it shall be.

Mental attitude is an important factor in the maintenance of sound physical health. All doctors know, and most of them will admit, that the patient's mental attitude is more important in curing physical ailments than any other single factor.

Mental attitude is a determining factor—perhaps *the most important factor*—as to what results one gets from prayer. It has long been known that when one goes to prayer in a mental attitude swayed by fear, doubt, and anxiety, nothing but negative results are experienced. Only the prayers which are backed by a mental attitude of profound FAITH can be expected to bring positive results.

Your mental attitude while driving an automobile on the public highway determines very largely whether you are a safe driver or a traffic hazard endangering your own life and the lives of others. Most automobile accidents are said to happen because of drunk driving, anger, or some form of overanxiety or worry on the part of drivers.

Your mental attitude determines, to a large extent, whether you find peace of mind or go through life in a state of frustration and misery.

Mental attitude is the warp and the woof of all salesmanship, regardless of what one is selling—merchandise, personal services, or any commodity. A person with a negative mental attitude can sell nothing. He may take an order from someone who buys something from him, but no *selling* was done. The transaction was entirely one of *buying*. Perhaps you have seen the truth demonstrated in many retail stores where the minds of the salespeople clearly were not directed toward pleasing the customers.

Mental attitude controls, very largely, the space one occupies in life, the success one achieves, the friends one makes, and the contributions one makes to posterity. It would be no great overstatement of the truth if said that mental attitude is EVERYTHING.

Mental attitude is the means by which one may condition his mind to go through surgery or dentistry without fear of physical pain. The means by which this can be accomplished are clearly described in subsequent chapters.

There are some who believe that one's mental attitude while occupying the physical body during life influences what happens to one after death. There is no positive proof of this theory except that it is obviously logical.

Last, the most convincing evidence of the importance of mental attitude is the fact that it is *the one and only thing* over which anyone has been given complete, unchallengeable privilege of personal control. We cannot control the thoughts or the actions of other people. We cannot control either our coming in or going out of life, but we do have the inexorable privilege of controlling every thought we release from our minds, from the time we begin to think to the time that life is ended.

Here then is the most profound, the most significant of all facts which influence an individual's life! It is logical that by giving every person the complete control over his thinking the

Creator intended this to be a priceless asset, and it is precisely that because the mind is the one and only means by which an individual may plan his own life and live it as he chooses.

William E. Henley, the poet, must have understood this great truth when he wrote the lines, "I am the Master of my Fate, I am the Captain of my Soul." Truly, we may become the captain of our worldly destiny precisely to the extent that we take possession of our own minds and direct them to definite ends through control of our mental attitude.

Mental Attitude Can Be Negative or Positive

Only a positive mental attitude pays off in the affairs of our everyday living, so let us see what it is, and how we may get it and apply it in the struggle for the things and circumstances we desire in life.

A positive mental attitude has many facets and uncountable combinations for its application in connection with every circumstance which affects our lives.

First of all, a positive mental attitude is the fixed purpose to make every experience, whether it is pleasant or unpleasant, yield some form of benefit which will help us balance our lives with all the things which lead to peace of mind.

It is the habit of searching for "the seed of an equivalent benefit" which comes with every failure, defeat, or adversity we experience, and causing that seed to germinate into something beneficial. Only a positive mental attitude can recognize and benefit by the lessons or the seed of an equivalent benefit which comes with all unpleasant things which one experiences.

A positive mental attitude is the habit of keeping the mind busily engaged in connection with the circumstances and things one desires in life, and *off* the things one does not desire. The majority of people go all the way through life with their mental attitude dominated by fears, and anxieties, and worries over circumstances which somehow have way of making their appearance sooner or later. And the strange part of this truth is that these people often blame other people for the misfortunes they have thus brought upon themselves by their negative mental attitudes.

The mind has a definite way of clothing one's thoughts in appropriate physical equivalents. Think in terms of poverty and you will live in poverty. Think in terms of opulence and you will attract it. *Through the eternal law of harmonious attraction one's thoughts always clothe themselves in material things appropriate unto their nature.*

A positive mental attitude is the habit of looking upon all unpleasant circumstances with which one meets as merely opportunity for one to test his capacity to rise above them by searching for that "seed of an equivalent benefit" and putting it to work.

A positive mental attitude is the habit of evaluating all problems and distinguishing the difference between those one can master and those one cannot control. The person with a positive mental attitude endeavors to solve the problems he can control and so relates himself to those he cannot control that they do not influence his mental attitude from positive to negative.

A positive mental attitude helps one make allowances for the frailties and weaknesses of other people without becoming shocked by their negative-mindedness or being influenced by their way of thinking.

It is the habit of acting with definiteness of purpose with full belief in both the soundness of that purpose and one's ability to achieve it.

It is the habit of going beyond the letter of one's responsibility and rendering more service and better service than one is obligated to render, and doing it in a friendly, pleasing manner.

It is the habit of choosing a definite goal and marching forward toward its attainment without hesitating because of either commendation or condemnation.

It is the habit of looking for the good qualities in other people and expecting to find them, and then being prepared to recognize unfavorable qualities without being shocked into a negative state of mind.

It is the habit of mastering all the emotions by submitting them to examination by the head and the discipline of the power of will.

It is the habit of facing all the facts which affect one's life, both the pleasant and the unpleasant, and keeping a cool head when unpleasant emergencies arise.

It is recognition of the universal power of Infinite Intelligence and the knowledge that it can be appropriated and directed to the attainment of definite ends through the medium of FAITH.

A positive mental attitude is the chief medium by which Alcoholics Anonymous have helped countless numbers of men and women to cure themselves of alcoholism. And it is also the basis of curing the habit of excessive smoking.

It is the medium of all forms of "mind-conditioning" for whatsoever purposes, including the elimination of all types of fear.

All habits, good or bad, voluntary or involuntary, are established by one's mental attitude. It is the medium by which one may transmute unpleasant habits and circumstances into some form of benefit.

A positive mental attitude is the sole medium by which one may exercise the inherent right to maintain complete control over his own mind, without help or hindrance from anyone. And it is the means by which stumbling blocks may be transmuted into stepping stones of progress in every calling.

Mental attitude reveals itself from one person to another, without spoken words, signs, or actions, by the medium of telepathy; therefore, it is contagious.

One's mental attitude while eating aids digestion or retards it, and or negative mental attitude can paralyze the digestive forces altogether.

The mental attitude of a public speaker often determines how his speech is interpreted, even more effectively than the words he uses. And the mental attitude of a writer while he is writing always is conveyed to the reader, behind the lines of his writing.

By the proper conditioning and control of the mental attitude, one may condition his mind to meet any sort of unpleasant circumstance without becoming upset by it, including even the emergency of death of loved ones.

Mental attitude is a two-way gate across the pathway of life which can be swung one way into success and the other way into failure. The tragedy is that most people swing the gate in the wrong direction.

The patient's mental attitude is the doctor's best aid or his greatest hindrance in the treatment of physical ailments, depending upon whether the attitude is positive or negative.

From these statements of known facts one can easily understand why *mental attitude is everything,* because it influences every experience with which we meet, *and it is under our complete control at all times.*

What a profound thought it is to recognize that the one thing which can give us success or bring us failure, bless us with peace of mind or curse us with misery all the days of our lives, is simply the privilege of taking possession of our own minds and guiding them to whatever ends we choose, through our mental attitude.

HOW CAN ONE CONTROL THE MENTAL ATTITUDE?

The starting point of control of the mental attitude is motive and desire. No one ever does anything without a motive or motives, and the stronger the motive the easier it is to control the mental attitude.

Mental attitude can be influenced and controlled by a number of factors, among them, these:

1. By a BURNING DESIRE for the attainment of a definite purpose based upon one or more of the nine basic motives which activate all human endeavor. (See the list of the nine basic motives in Chapter 4.)
2. By conditioning the mind to automatically choose and carry out definite positive objectives, with the aid of the EIGHT GUIDING PRINCES, or some similar technique which will keep the mind busily engaged with

positive objectives, when one is asleep as well as when one is awake. (See description of the nature of the EIGHT GUIDING PRINCES in Chapter 7.)

3. By close association with people who inspire active engagement in positive purposes, and refusal to be influenced by negative-minded people.
4. By auto-suggestion through which the mind is constantly given positive directives until it attracts only that for which these directives call.
5. By a profound recognition and its adoption and use, of the individual's exclusive privilege of controlling and directing his own mind.
6. By the aid of a machine by which the subconscious mind can be given directives while one sleeps.

Our great American Way of Life, our matchless system of free enterprise, and the personal liberty of which we feel so proud are nothing more than the mental attitude of people organized and directed to specialized ends.

The one factor of the American Way of Life which stands out boldly above all others consists in the laws and the mechanisms of government we have set up to protect the individual in the freedom of control over his mental attitude.

It was this freedom of control over mental attitude which gave us the great leaders who patterned our American Way of Life and our great system of free enterprise. *And it is significant that only those who moved with a positive mental attitude became leaders.*

Thomas A. Edison's positive mental attitude sustained him through more than ten thousand failures and led him to the discovery of the incandescent electric light, which ushered in the great electrical age and the fabulous riches it gave us.

Henry Ford's positive mental attitude kept him afloat during his early struggles in building the first automobile, and it served as his greatest and most important asset in establishing the fabulous industrial empire which made him richer than Croesus and provided employment, directly and indirectly, for perhaps more than ten million men and women.

Andrew Carnegie's positive mental attitude lifted him up from poverty and obscurity and served as his major asset in the establishment of an industry which gave birth to the great steel age, which now serves as the most important link in our entire economic system.

Mahatma Gandhi's positive mental attitude (he called it passive resistance) was more than a match for the great power of the British military forces, which ruled India for many generations. It was Gandhi's positive mental attitude which brought together a Master Mind alliance of more than two hundred million of his fellowmen who gave mighty power to his "passive resistance" and freed India from British control without the firing of a gun or the loss of single soldier.

It was the positive mental attitude of the builder of the great Golden Gate suspension bridge which gave us the world's longest single-span bridge, despite the fact that his first attempt indicated that the job was an engineering impossibility and the state officials turned thumbs down on it by withholding the necessary initial funds for the work.

Wherever we find leadership and great achievement at any level of life, in any calling or occupation, we recognize that it is founded upon a positive mental attitude.

A positive mental attitude is the sum total of hopes, wishes, and beliefs, added up and transmuted into FAITH! And Faith is the open door to Infinite Intelligence, which can be appropriated and used *only by those who maintain a positive mental attitude.*

And the most profound fact regarding a positive mental attitude is that everyone has the privilege of adopting it and using it for all purposes, *without money and without price.*

The secret by which this profound truth may enrich your mind and give you mastery over obstacles of happiness which you may encounter the remainder of your life have been revealed in the chapters which follow.

Head in with an open mind, and you will be rewarded with a form of riches sufficient to give you a well-balanced life, freedom from fear, and peace of mind which shall endure. In the chapters which follow you will be introduced to the greatest person now living. When you discover the name of this person, turn down a glass, mark the page where the name was revealed, and sign it, for you will have discovered a new meaning of the purpose for which we are on this earth plane for the brief span of years called Life.

"When riches begin to come, they come so quickly and in such great abundance that one wonders where they have been hiding all those lean years."

—*Think and Grow Rich*

The Second Miracle of Life

THE LAW OF GROWTH THROUGH ETERNAL CHANGE

ETERNAL CHANGE is the one Miracle of Life most bitterly opposed by the vast majority of the human race. And failure to understand it and adapt one's self to it is the major cause of all personal failures and defeats.

The changes in our way of living have revealed during the first half of the twentieth century more of Nature's secrets than had been uncovered during the entire past of civilization. Among these have been the discovery of the automobile, the talking machine, radio, television, talking pictures, airplanes, radar, and wireless telegraphy, all produced by ever-changing processes of the human mind.

Change is the tool of human progress, in the affairs of nations no less than in the lives of individuals. And the business or industry which neglects to keep moving forward through change is doomed to failure.

The great American Way of Life, which has provided the people with the highest standard of living the world has ever known, has been the product of continuous change.

The Law of Change is one of Nature's inexorable laws, without which there could have been no such reality as civilization. Without the law of change, the human race would still be where it started from—on the plane with all the other animals and creatures of the earth which are eternally bound and limited by a pattern of instinct, beyond which they never can rise.

Through the Law of Change (popularly known as evolution) the human race has slowly left the baseline of the animal family, where the destiny of all living things was fixed by a life pattern of instinct, and has evolved into higher and still higher degrees of intelligence, until man now is something infinitely greater than the thirty thousand man-made gods whom he has created and worshiped since the beginning of his long and tortuous trip upward.

The entire history of mankind, the record of life in all its forms, is a clearly marked pattern of perpetual change. No living thing is the same two minutes in succession, and this change is so inexorable that the entire physical body of man undergoes a complete change, and a replacement of all the physical cells of the body, every seven months.

The Law of Change is the Creator's device for separating man from the remainder of the animalistic families. It is also the device by which the eternal varieties of life, the habits and the thoughts of men, are continuously reshaping themselves into a better system of human relations leading toward harmony and better understanding among man. And it is one of the devices one must use in mastering fixed habits which cause the fear of physical pain.

Through the Law of Change the habits of men, which do not conform to the overall pattern and purpose of the universe, are periodically broken up by wars, epidemics of disease, droughts, and other irresistible forces of Nature which force man to free himself from the effects of his follies and start all over again. And this same Law of Change which levels the peoples of all nations to the baseline of the overall plan of the universe *applies, with equal force, to individuals who fail to interpret and adapt themselves to Nature's laws.*

"Conform to the overall plan or perish," is Nature's warning!

The fears and the failures of men, the shocks and disappointments in human relations, all are designed to shake men loose from habits to which he so tenaciously clings, *so he may adapt, embrace, and benefit by better habits of growth.*

The whole purpose of education, or so it should be at least, is to start the mind of the individual to growing and developing *from within*, to cause the mind to evolve and expand through constant changes in the thinking process so that the individual may eventually become acquainted with his own potential powers and thereby be capable of solving his personal problems.

Evidence that this theory conforms with Nature's plans may be found in the fact that the better educated people of all times are those who graduate from the great UNIVERSITY OF HARD KNOCKS, through experiences which *force them to develop and use their mind power.*

The Law of Change is the greatest of all sources of education! Understand this truth and you will no longer oppose the changes which give you a wider scope of understanding of yourself and the world at large. And you will no longer resist Nature's breaking up of some of the habits you have formed *which have not brought you peace of mind or material riches.*

The traits the Creator must emphatically frown upon in human beings are complacency, self-satisfaction, procrastination, fear, and self-imposed limitations, all of which carry heavy penalties which are exacted from those who indulge them.

Through the Law of Change man is forced to keep on growing. Whenever a nation, a business institution, or an individual ceases to change and settles into a rut of routine habits, some mysterious power enters and smashes the setup, breaks up the old habits, and lays the foundation for new and better habits. *In everything and everyone the law of growth is through eternal change!*

Flexibility of personality—the capacity of an individual to adapt himself to all circumstances which affect his life—is one of the major factors of an attractive personality. Also, it is the medium of adaptability to the great law of growth through change.

The Ford Motor Company was pyramided from the humble beginning of a one-room brick factory into one of the world's greatest industrial empires, which provides directly and indirectly, employment for hundreds of thousands of people. Henry Ford, the founder, despite all his traits of genius in industrial management, very nearly wrecked the business on at least two occasions because his capacity for flexibility—the ability to change—had not kept up with his years. After his death the business was taken over by his grandson, a mere youth in comparison with the founder of the business, but a young man with a great flexibility and willingness to follow the law of growth through change. In a matter of a few years the young man transformed the Ford industrial empire into an institution far in advance of anything his grandfather had accomplished during his entire lifetime.

In labor relations, in industrial management, in automobile designing and styling, young Henry Ford proved himself to be a man who invited change instead of fighting it, and by this application of wisdom made himself an industrial wizard overnight.

On every hand the soul of man cries out, saying in effect: Wake up, get wise to yourself, throw off your old habits before they bind you in chains and force you to come back for another try at life through a new incarnation. If you wish to finish the job while you are here, you must adapt yourself to the great Law of Change and continue growing.

The soul of man cries out in words of warning and says: Everything, every circumstance which touches your life, whether it be pleasant or unpleasant, is grist for your Mill of Life. Embrace it as such, grind it into your chosen pattern of living, and let it serve instead of tormenting you through fear and worry.

An old Virginia family was born and reared in the mountains of southwest Virginia, in comparative poverty. At long last the railroads came and the rich coal fields were put into operation. This family sold their mountain land for a fabulous sum, moved into town, and built a new modern home. When the house was completed, with three bathrooms equipped with all modern conveniences, the wife refused to permit the contractor to be paid because she claimed the job had not been finished.

"What," the contractor enquired, "is missing?"

"You know well enough what is missing," the wife replied. "There is no back-house on the place."

"Well," explained the surprised contractor, "back-houses went out of style when you moved to town. You now have three beautiful bathrooms where you can perform all your necessary bodily attentions in private and with great comfort."

"All my life," the wife exclaimed, "I have enjoyed reading Sears and Roebuck's catalogue in my back-house and I have no intention of giving up this pleasure at my age. Build that back-house or you get no money."

The back-house was built! When the wife went down to inspect it, she screamed, "It will not do! It has only one hole in the seat and we have always been used to two holes."

So another hole was provided, and for good measure the contractor installed plumbing for hot and cold water, and also a telephone, so the rich old lady could attend to all her social duties while reading her Sears and Roebuck catalogue in the back-house.

Complacency and old habits had won a victory over change and progress.

When cash registers were first introduced, the manufacturers had great difficulty in getting merchants to install them, and salespeople in general went into spasms over them. Store clerks frowned upon the new device as being a suggestion that they were dishonest, and merchants protested that the cost of the machines, plus the time required for their operation, would eat too deeply into their profits.

But the Law of Change is persistent and inevitable! Today no merchant in his right mind would try to operate a retail business, in which anyone but himself had to handle cash receipts, without the aid of the cash register.

When the Federal Reserve Banking System was forced into operation by the Congress of the United States, the bankers in general sent up a howl of protest. The system meant radical change which broke up their established ways of doing business. The Federal Reserve Banking System proved to be the greatest safeguard for the banks that was ever introduced, and today if it were suggested that the system be abolished, the bankers probably would put up an equally loud cry against the change.

Of the utmost significance is the fact that the Creator provided man with the one and only means by which he has broken away from the animal family and ascended into spiritual estates, where he may be the master of his own earthly fate. The means thus provided is the Law of Change. By the simple process of changing his mental attitude, man can draw for himself any pattern of life and living he chooses and make that pattern a reality. This is the one and only thing over which man has been provided with irrevocable, unchallenged, and unchallengeable powers of absolute control—a fact which suggests that it must have been considered by the Creator to be the most important prerogative of man.

Dictators and would-be world conquerors come and they go. They always go because it is not a part of the overall plan of the universe for man to be subjugated. But it is a part of the eternal pattern that every man shall be free, to live his own life his own way, to control his thoughts and his deeds, to make his own earthly destiny.

That is why the philosopher, who looks backward into the past to determine what is going to happen in the yet unborn future, cannot get excited because a Hitler or a Stalin momentarily basks in the light of his own ego and threatens the freedom of mankind. For these men, like all others of their ilk who have preceded them, will destroy themselves with their own excesses and vanities and their lusts for power over the free world. Moreover, these would-be stranglers of human freedom may be only demons who unwittingly serve as shock troops to awaken man from his complacency and make way for the change that will bring new and better ways of living.

Nature lends man through change after change by peaceful means as long as man cooperates, but resorts to revolutionary methods if man rebels and neglects or refuses to conform to the Law of Change. The revolutionary method may consist in the death of a loved one or a severe illness; it may bring a failure in business, or the loss of a job, which forces the individual to change his occupation and seek employment in an entirely new field, where he will find greater opportunities he would never have known if his old habits had not been broken up.

Nature enforces the law of fixation of habits in every living thing lower than man, and just as definitely as it enforces the Law of Change in the habits of man, nature thus provides the only means by which man may grow and evolve in accordance with his fixed position in the overall plan of the universe.

Thomas A. Edison's first major adversity was experienced when his teacher sent him home after only three months in a graded school, with a note to his parents saying he did not have the capacity to take an education. He never went back to school—a conventional school, that is—but he began to school himself in the great University of Hard Knocks, where he gained an education which made him the greatest inventor of all times. Before he was graduated from university, he was fired from one job after another, while the hand of Destiny guided him through *the essential changes* which prepared him to become a great inventor. A formal schooling perhaps would have spoiled his chances of becoming great.

Nature knows what she is about when adversity, physical pain, sorrow, distress, failure, and temporary defeat overtake one. Remember this and profit by it the next time you meet with adversity. And instead of crying out in anger, or shivering with fear, hold high your head and look in all directions for that seed of an equivalent benefit which is carried in every circumstance of adversity.

I am never frightened by revolutionary changes in my life, whether they are voluntary, or forced upon me by circumstances of an unpleasant nature over which I have no control, *for I do at least have control over my reaction to these circumstances.* And I exercise this privilege, not by complaining, but by searching for that seed of an equivalent benefit which each experience carries with it.

The book you are reading is literally the product of over forty years of continuous and oftentimes drastic changes I have had to make in my way of life. Many of the changes were forced, some of them were voluntary, but all of them added up, at long last, to the revelation of the secret of peace of mind and material prosperity which has been so definitely defined through this volume.

When I was commissioned by Andrew Carnegie to begin research in preparation for the organization of the world's first practical philosophy of person achievement, I was so little prepared for the job that truthfully I did not know the real meaning of the word "philosophy" until I looked it up in a dictionary.

If ever anyone began a job by starting from scratch, I began right there! What I had to do to prepare myself for the successful fulfillment of the assignment Mr. Carnegie had given me was not mere change, it was practically a *complete rebuilding job*! Perhaps this was fortunate because the knowledge I gained from my own personal struggles led eventually to the revelation of the supreme "miracle" which is the central purpose in writing this volume.

And the rebuilding job included the changing of self-made habits of failure for self-made habits of success, which at long last gave me a balanced life that included everything I desire or need for the style of living I have chosen.

Among other changes I had to make in preparation for my life work were these:

1. Curing of the habit of selling myself short because of lack of self-confidence.

2. Freeing myself from the habit of yielding to the seven basic fears, including the fear of ill health and physical pain.

3. Removing the habit of binding myself to penury and want by my self-imposed limitations.

4. Breaking the habit of neglect in taking possession of my own mind and directing it to the attainment of all my desires.

5. Curing myself of the habit of failure to relate to fame and freedom from want, in a spirit of humble gratitude.

6. Changing the habit of expecting to reap before I have sown. (Confusing my NEEDS with my RIGHTS to receive.)

7. Curing myself of the false belief that HONESTY and SINCERITY OF PURPOSE, alone, will lead to success.

8. Changing the false belief that EDUCATION comes only through the media of higher learning.

9. Correcting the habit of neglecting to schedule my life on a practical budget and use of TIME.

10. Curing myself of the habit of failure to devote the major portion of my TIME to the pursuit of my Definite Major Purpose in life.

11. Changing my habit of impatience.

12. Correcting the habit of failure to take inventory of all my intangible riches and express gratitude for them.

13. Correction of the habit of endeavoring to accumulate more material riches than I could legitimately use.

14. Correcting the habit of believing it is more beneficial to RECEIVE than to GIVE.

15. Last, but not least, correcting the habit of neglect in recognizing the source of Infinite Intelligence and the means of contacting and using it for any desired purpose by application of the SUPREME MIRACLE.

These do not represent the entire list of changes I had to make in my habits of thought and action, but they are some of the more important ones, from which it will be obvious that the LAW OF CHANGE has played an important part in my life, and just as obvious that had I not made these changes I would have deprived myself of the privilege of giving the world a workable philosophy of personal success which has brought me more fame and recognition than one person needs on this plane of life.

In presenting these intimate circumstances of my life thus, frankly I hope you will recognize that I am preparing you to accept the truth that perhaps you, too, will need to change some of your habits before you may enjoy a full, well-balanced life made to your own pattern and style of living.

The extent to which you will need to make changes in your present habits is entirely something you will have to decide, but the list must include the mastery of the seven basic fears if you aspire to the attainment of a well-balanced life which includes peace of mind.

The seven basic fears are as follows:

1. The Fear of POVERTY.
2. The Fear of CRITICISM.
3. The Fear of ILL HEALTH and PHYSICAL PAIN.
4. The Fear of the LOSS of LOVE.
5. The Fear of the LOSS of LIBERTY.
6. The Fear of OLD AGE.
7. The Fear of DEATH.

In the chapters which follow you will be given instructions for the mastery of these and all other fears, through the application of new habits of thinking which you must develop and use in the place of the old habits which have made these fears possible. Whatever other changes may be necessary to give you a well rounded out life will not alter the fact that mastery of these seven basic fears is a "must" in your rebuilding program.

Take heart from the promise that these correction instructions will impose upon you no hardships nor actions beyond your ability to control. They have a price attached to them, but it is a price well within the means of all normal people.

We are where we are and what we are because of our daily habits!

Our habits are under our individual control, and they may be changed at any time by the mere will to change them. This prerogative is the one and only privilege over which the individual has complete control. Habits are made by our thinking, and our thinking is the one thing over which the Creator gave us complete right of control, and along with this right, profound rewards for our exercising the right, and terrible penalties for our failure to exercise it.

"When defeat comes, accept it as a signal that your plans are not sound, rebuild those plans, and set sail once more toward your coveted goal."

—*Think and Grow Rich*

The Third
Miracle of Life

THE NECESSITY OF GROWTH
THROUGH STRUGGLE

THE NECESSITY FOR STRUGGLE is one of the clever devices through which Nature forces individuals to expand, develop, progress, and become strong through resistances. Struggle can, and it does, become either an ordeal or a magnificent experience through which the individual expresses gratitude, for the opportunity to conquer the cause of his struggle.

Life, from birth until death, is literally an unbroken record of an ever-increasing variety of which no individual can avoid. Mastery of ignorance calls for struggle. Education involves eternal struggle, and every day is "commencement" day because education is cumulative: it is a lifetime job.

The accumulation of material riches abounds in the necessity from struggle; so much so, in fact, that many individuals actually kill themselves early in life due to anxiety and overexertion in the effort to acquire more money than they need.

Maintenance of sound physical health calls for eternal struggle with the multifarious enemies of sound health, struggle for food and shelter, struggle for an opportunity to earn a living, struggle to hold a job, struggle to gain recognition in a profession, struggle to keep a business out of bankruptcy.

Look in whatever direction we may, and we find that there is hardly a circumstance of daily life which does not call for individual struggle in order to survive.

We are forced to recognize that this great universal necessity for struggle must, and it does, have a definite and useful purpose. That purpose is to force the individual to sharpen his wits, arouse his enthusiasm, build up his spirit of Faith, gain Definiteness of Purpose, develop his power of will, inspire his faculty of imagination to give him new uses for old ideas and concepts, *and thereby fulfill some unknown mission for which he may have been born.*

Struggle keeps man from going to sleep with self-satisfaction or laziness, and force him onward and upward in the fulfillment of his mission in life, and he thereby makes his individual contribution to whatever may be the great Universal Purpose of mankind on earth.

Strength, both physical and spiritual, is the product of struggle! "Do the thing," said Emerson, "and you shall have the power." Meet struggle and master it, says Nature, and you shall have *strength and wisdom sufficient for all your needs.*

For twenty odd years I was forced to struggle in mastering the problems incidental to my work in organizing the world's first practical philosophy of success. First, I was forced to struggle in preparing myself with the necessary knowledge to produce the philosophy. Second, I was forced to struggle to maintain myself economically while doing the research necessary to produce the philosophy. Then I set with still greater necessities for struggle while gaining recognition from the world for myself and the philosophy.

Twenty years of struggle without any direct financial compensation is an experience not calculated to give one sustained hope, but it was the price I had to pay for a philosophy which was destined to benefit millions of people, many of whom were not born when I began my work.

Discouraging? Heartbreaking? Not at all! For I recognized from the beginning that out of my struggle would come triumph and victory in proportion to the labors invested in my task. In this hope I have not been disappointed, but I have been overwhelmed with the bountiful manner in which the world has responded and paid me tribute for the long years of struggle that went into my work.

Also, I have gained from my struggle something of still greater and more profound value. It is recognition that through my struggles *I have reached deeply* into the spiritual wells of my soul, and there I have found powers available for every purpose I may desire; powers I never knew I possessed, and *never would have discovered except by the means of struggle*!

Through my struggles I discovered and learned how to make practical use of the magical eight Princes of guidance described in Chapter 7—the unseen friends who administer to all my physical, financial, and spiritual needs, who work for me while I sleep and I am awake.

Also, it was through struggles that the great Law of Cosmic Habitforce (the law that is the fixer of all habits, the comptroller of all natural laws) was revealed to me, the law which led me, at long last, to where I was ready to give the world the benefit of my experience from struggle.

There may be some pain in most forms of struggle, but Nature compensates the individual for the pain in the form of *power and strength and wisdom which come from practical experience.*

While organizing the Science of Success philosophy, I made the revealing discovery that all the more successful leaders, in every calling, in every profession and every walk of life, had gained their leadership in almost exact ratio to the extent of their struggles in the attainment of their leadership.

And I observed, with profound interest, that no man, who had not been thoroughly tested by the necessity of struggle seemed ever to have been chosen as a leader in times of great crisis during the interim between the stone age and our present-day civilization.

Careful study of the entire record of civilization itself, from the age of the cave man to the present, shows clearly that it is the product of eternal struggle. Yes, struggle definitely is one of the Creator's devices for forcing individuals to respond to the Law of Change in order that the overall plan of the universe may be carried out.

When any individual reconciles himself to the state of mind wherein he is willing to accept largesse from government, instead of supplying his needs through personal initiative, that individual is on the road to decay and spiritual blindness. When a majority of the people of any nation give up their inherited prerogative right to make their own way through struggle, *history shows clearly that the entire nation is in a tailspin of decay that inevitable must end in extinction.*

And the individual who not only is willing to live on the public treasury, *but demands that he be fed from it,* is already dead spiritually. The physical body still walks but it is nothing but an empty shell whose only hope for the future is a funeral. This, of course, has reference only to able-bodied people who quit the struggle because they are too indifferent or too lazy to keep on growing through the Law of Change and the urge to struggle.

If you wish a strong arm, says Nature, give it systematic use under the weight of a three-pound hammer and soon you will have muscles like bands of steel. If you do not wish a strong arm, says Nature, tie it in a sling, take it out of use, and remove the cause for struggle, and its strength will wither and die.

In every form of life, atrophy and death come from idleness! The one thing Nature will not tolerate is idleness. Through the necessity for struggle and the Law of Change Nature keeps everything throughout the universe in a constant state of flux. Nothing, from the electrons and protons of matter to the suns and planets which float throughout space, is ever still for a single second. Nature's motto is keep moving or perish! There is no halfway ground, no compromise, no exceptions for any reason whatsoever.

And should you doubt that Nature intends for every individual to keep struggling or perish, observe what takes place with the person who makes his fortune and "retires," gives up the struggle because he no longer believes it is necessary.

The strongest trees are not those in heavily protected forests, but the trees which stand in open spaces where they are in constant struggle with wind and sun and all the elements of weather.

My grandfather was a wagon maker. In clearing his land for the production of crops he always left a few oak trees standing in the open fields, where they could be toughened by the exposure. These he used for the "fellows" needed in making wagon wheels—timber that could be bent into arc-shaped segments without breaking in the process. He found that trees protected by the forest could not produce the sort of timber he required. It was too soft and brittle because it had not been under the necessity of struggle; the selfsame reason why some people are "soft" and unprepared to cope with the resistance of life.

Most people go through life by the line of least resistance in every circumstance where they can make a choice. They do not recognize *that following the line of least resistance makes all rivers and some men crooked*!

From my experience with struggle I discovered that the Creator never singles out an individual for an important service to mankind without first testing him through struggle, in proportion to the nature of the service he is to render. Thus through struggle I learned to interpret the laws, purposes, and working plans of the Creator as they related to me and to mankind in general.

What greater benefits could anyone desire from struggle?

What greater rewards could anyone gain from any other cause?

Briefly we have reviewed only three of Life's Miracles, but these are by no means the more important of the miracles we are to inspect in our trip through Nature's Wonderland Valley.

However, we have witnessed enough on our trip to convince us that there is good in all circumstances which touch or influence our lives, whether they be circumstances over which we have complete control or those over which we have no control *except the control of our mental reaction to them.*

As we proceed on our trip, through the chapters to follow, our minds should unfold until we recognize that circumstances which we may regard as unpleasant may be a part of the Creator's overall plan in connection with human destiny on this earth. The major purpose of this chapter is to broaden the mind so it may encompass and envision important facts of life *outside of those which immediately concern* the individual.

Peace of mind is not possible without this capacity for panoramic vision of the entire picture and purpose of life. We must recognize that our individual incarnation, through which we are tossed into this material world without ceremony and without our consent, was for a purpose above and beyond our individual pleasures and desires.

Once we understand this broader purpose of life, we come reconciled to the experience of struggle we must undergo while passing this way, and we accept them as circumstances of opportunity through which we may prepare ourselves for still higher and better planes of existence than the one on which we now dwell.

"Poverty needs no plan. It needs no one to aid it, because it is bold and ruthless."

—*Think and Grow Rich*

The Fourth
Miracle of Life

THE MASTERY OF POVERTY

POVERTY is the result of a negative condition of the mind, which practically every living person experiences at one time or another. It is the first and the most disastrous of the seven basic fears, but it is only a state of mind, and like the other six it is subject to the control of the individual.

The fact that a major portion of all people are born in surroundings of poverty, *accept it as inescapable*, and go with it all through their lives indicates how potent a factor it is in the lives of people. It may well be that poverty is one of the testing devices with which the Creator separates the weak from the strong, for it is a notable fact that those who master poverty become rich not only in material things, *but also rich and often wise in spiritual values as well*.

I have observed that men who have mastered poverty invariably have a keen sense of Faith in their ability to master practically everything else which stands in the way of their progress; while those who have accepted poverty as inescapable show signs of weaknesses in many other directions. In no case have I known anyone who had accepted poverty as unavoidable, who had not failed also to exercise that Great Gift of the power to take possession of his mind power (as the Creator intended all people should do).

All people go through testing periods throughout their lives, under many circumstances, which clearly disclose whether or not they have accepted and used that Great Gift of exclusive control over their own mind power. And I have observed that along with this Great Gift from the Infinite goes, also, definite penalties for neglect to embrace and use the Gift, and definite rewards for its recognition and use.

One of the more important rewards for its use consists in complete freedom from the entire seven basic fears and all the lesser fears, with full access to the magic power of FAITH to take the place of these fears.

The penalties for neglect to embrace and use this Great Gift are legion. In addition to all of the seven basic fears, there are many other liabilities not included with these fears. One of the major penalties for failure to use the Great Gift is *the total impossibility of attaining peace of mind.*

Poverty has many merits if and when an individual relates himself to it in a positive mental attitude instead of submitting to it in the false belief it is unavoidable, or the lazy attitude that it is not worth fighting off. Poverty may be one of the devices with which the Creator forces man to sharpen his wits, arouse his enthusiasm, act on his personal initiative, and make a determined fight against the forces which oppose him, in order that he may survive.

Poverty may also be a device of the Creator by which he maneuvers man into a state of mind where he finally *discovers himself from within*. In a great country like the United States of America there is no valid reason for any able-bodied person to accept and become bound to servitude through poverty. Here, as nowhere else in the world, is a training ground for personal freedom, which offers every individual the best of all possible opportunities to embrace and use this Great Gift of *the right to pattern his own earthly destiny and attain it*. And here, as nowhere else, has the individual been provided with every conceivable motive for embracing and using the Great Gift. The payoff is so great that the individual may literally "write his own ticket."

The best evidence that the hand of Destiny smiles on those who are born to poverty consists in the well-recognized fact that too seldom does an individual, who is born to great wealth, ever contribute any worthy contributions to the world which makes it a better place for mankind. Many children of very rich people, who never have the benefit of the seasoning influence of poverty, often grow up "soft," and lacking in the necessary endurance or the motive to make themselves useful.

When Fortune does smile upon a person who has great wealth, she generally chooses only those who created their wealth through useful services, not those who inherited it or procured it through means which injured others. Fortune definitely frowns upon all ill-gotten wealth *and often causes it to mysteriously evaporate*.

Whether poverty becomes a curse or a blessing depends entirely upon the way the individual relates himself to it. If it is accepted in a spirit of meekness, as an unavoidable handicap, then it becomes just that. If poverty is accepted as a mere challenge to the individual to fight his way through it and master it, then it becomes a blessing; in fact, one of the great miracles of life. Poverty may become either a stumbling block over which the individual dashes to pieces his hope of personal freedom or a stepping stone on which he may rise to whatever heights of achievement he may set his heart upon, depending entirely on his attitude toward it *and his reactions to it.*

Both poverty and riches consist in a state of the mind! They follow precisely the pattern the individual creates and visualizes by the dominating thoughts he expresses. Thoughts of poverty attract their material counterpart. Thoughts of riches likewise attract their material counterparts. This great truth explains why the majority of people go all the way through their lives in misery and poverty; they allow their minds to fear misery and poverty, and their dominating thoughts are on those circumstances. The law of harmonious attraction takes over and brings them that *which they expect.*

When I was a small boy, I heard a very dramatic speech on the subject of poverty which made a lasting impression upon my mind, and I am sure that speech was responsible for my determination to master poverty despite the fact I had been born in poverty and had never known anything except poverty. The speech came from my stepmother shortly after she came to our home and took over one of the most forlorn, poverty-stricken places I have ever known.

The speech follows:

This place which we call a home is a disgrace to all of us and a handicap for our children. We are all able-bodied people, and there is no need for us to accept poverty when we know that it is the result of nothing but laziness or indifference.

If we stay here and accept the conditions under which we now live, our children will grow up and accept these conditions also. I do not like poverty; I have never accepted poverty as my lot and I shall not accept it now!

For the moment I do not know what our first step will be in our break for freedom from poverty, but this much I do know, we shall make that break successfully, no matter how long it may take or how many sacrifices we may have to make. I intend that our children shall have the advantage of good educations, but more than this, I intend that they shall be inspired with the ambition to master poverty.

Poverty is a disease which once it is accepted becomes a fixation which is hard to shake off.

It is no disgrace to be born in poverty but it most decidedly is a disgrace to accept this birthright as irrevocable.

We live in the richest and the greatest country civilization has yet produced. Here opportunity beckons to everyone who has the ambition to recognize and embrace it, and as far as this family is concerned, if opportunity does not beckon to it we shall create our own opportunity to escape this sort of life.

Poverty is like creeping paralysis! Slowly it destroys the desire for freedom, strips one of the ambition to enjoy the better things in life, and undermines personal initiative. Also, it conditions one's mind for the acceptance of myriad fears, including the fear of ill health, the fear of criticism, and the fear of physical pain.

*Our children are too young to know the dangers of
accepting poverty as their lot, but I shall see to it that they
are made conscious of these dangers, and I shall see to
it also that they become prosperity conscious,* that they
expect prosperity and become willing to pay the price of
prosperity.

I have quoted the speech from memory, but it is substantially what my stepmother said to my father in my presence, shortly after they were married. That "first step" in the break from poverty, which she mentioned in her speech came when my stepmother inspired my father to enter Louisville Dental College and become a dentist and paid for his training with the life insurance money she received from the death of her first husband. With the income from that investment in my father, she sent her three children and my younger brother through college and started each of them on the road to mastery of poverty.

As for myself, she was instrumental in placing me in a position where the late Andrew Carnegie gave me an opportunity such as no other ever received, an opportunity which permitted me to learn from more than five hundred of the top-ranking men of who collaborated with me in giving the world its first practical philosophy of personal achievement, based on the know-how of my collaborators, gained from their lifetime experiences.

It is estimated that my personal contribution to posterity has already benefited more than sixty-five million people, throughout two-thirds of the world, the credit for which dates back to that historic speech of my stepmother's, in which she disavowed poverty.

We see, therefore, that poverty can be the means of inspiring one to plan and achieve profound objectives. She did not fear poverty, but she disliked it and refused to accept it, and somehow the Creator seems to favor those who know precisely what they want and what they do not want. My stepmother was one of that type. If she had accepted poverty, or had she feared poverty, the lines you are now reading never would have been written.

Poverty is a great experience, but it is something to experience and then master before it breaks the will to be free and independent. The person who has never experienced poverty is to be pitied, but the person who has experienced poverty and has accepted it as his lot is more to be pitied, for he has thereby condemned himself to eternal bondage.

Most of the truly great men and women throughout civilization have known poverty, but they experienced it, renounced it, mastered it, and made themselves free. Otherwise, they never would have become great. Anyone who accepts from life anything he does not want is not free. The Creator has provided everyone with the means of determining, very largely, his own earthly destiny, which consist in the privilege of taking possession of his own mind and directing it to the attainment of whatsoever ends he may desire. The reward for embracing and using this great prerogative is independence and freedom. The penalty for neglecting to embrace and use it is penury, want, and misery all the days of one's life. Could any truth be more clearly stated than this?

Poverty can be a profound blessing. It can also be a lifelong curse. The determining factor as to which it shall be consists in one's mental attitude toward it. If it is accepted as a challenge to greater effort, it is a blessing. If it is accepted as a challenge to greater effort, it is a blessing. If it is accepted as an unavoidable handicap, then it is an enduring curse.

Lately, remember that the fear of poverty brings with it a flock of related fears, including the fear of physical and mental pain.

I heard a story of a man who died and went to hell. During his entrance examination Satan asked, "What do you fear most?" To which the man replied, "I fear nothing." "Then," said Satan, "you are in the wrong place. *We accommodate only customers who are bound by fears.*"

Think of it! No place in hell for the person who has no fears.

I never hear the word "fear" that I do not think of a story told to me by Reuben Darby of the Massachusetts Mutual Life Insurance Company. When he was a small lad his uncle operated a grist mill on a Maryland plantation, on which a tenant family lived. One day a ten-year-old child of the family was sent down to the mill to request fifty cents of the plantation owner.

The owner looked up from his work, saw the child standing at a respectful distance, and demanded, "What do you want!?" Without moving from her tracks the child replied, "My mommy say send her fifty cents." In a threatening tone of voice and a scowl on his face, the owner of the mill yelled, "I'll do nothing of the sort! Now you run on back home or I will take a switch to you." And he went back to his work. In a little while he looked up again and saw the child still standing there. He grabbed a barrel stave, waved it toward the child, and said, "If you don't get out of here, I'll use this on you. Now get going before I—" But he did not finish the sentence, for by that time the child darted over in front of him, stuck her little face up toward him, and just screamed at the top of her voice, "My mommy's gotta have fifty cents!" Slowly the mill owner laid down the barrel stave, reached in his pocket, pulled out fifty cents, and handed it to the child. She grabbed the money quickly, backed off to the door, opened it, and then ran like a deer, while the mill owner stood with wide open eyes and mouth, pondering over the mysterious experience by which a child had subdued him and got away with it—*something people on his place were not supposed to do.*

Verily, fear can be transmuted into courage, a fact which the child demonstrated most convincingly.

Likewise, poverty can be transmuted into opulence and noteworthy achievements, a fact which my stepmother dramatically demonstrated by lifting our family out of both poverty and despair. She recognized that no person who *takes possession of his own mind and directs it to definite ends* needs to remain the victim of poverty or of anything else he does not desire.

Moving on that premise, which I inherited from my stepmother, I discovered the power of my own mind and took possession of it, and I have been blessed with the glorious privilege of introducing millions of men and women to the key with which they released themselves from their self-made prisons.

The difference between poverty and riches is not measurable in money or material possessions alone. There are twelve great riches, eleven of which are not material, but they are closely related to the spiritual forces available to mankind. In order that one may get a better idea of how to go about transmuting poverty into riches the twelve great riches are here briefly described.

THE TWELVE GREAT RICHES OF LIFE

1. A Positive Mental Attitude

A positive Mental Attitude heads the list of the Twelve Great Riches, because all riches, material or otherwise, begin as a state of mind, the one and only thing over which an individual has complete, inalienable power of control. One's mental attitude supplies the "pulling power" which attracts to him the material equivalent of all fears, desires, doubts, and beliefs. Mental attitude is also the factor which determines whether one's prayers bring negative or positive results. It is but little cause for wonder, therefore, that a positive mental attitude heads the list of all the great riches of life.

2. Sound Physical Health

Sound health begins with a "health consciousness," the product of a mind which thinks in terms of health and not in terms of illness, plus temperance and moderation in eating and in the balancing of physical activities. Maintenance of a positive mental attitude is one of the greatest forms of prevention of ill health known to mankind. It rates as "great" because it is under one's control and is subject at all times to one's direction to any desired end.

3. Harmony In Human Relations

There are two forms of harmony, both of which are required to entitle harmony to rank as one of the twelve great riches of life; namely, harmony with one's self and harmony with others. One's first responsibility is that of establishing harmony *within*. This calls for the mastery of fear, maintenance of a positive mental attitude, and the adoption of a major purpose in life behind which one can build an enduring faith in its achievement. Be at peace within your own soul, and you will have no difficulty in relating yourself in a spirit of harmony with others. Friction in human relations often is the result of confusion, frustration, fear, and doubt within the individual who, oftentimes, mirrors these negative states of mind in other people, thus making harmony impossible.

Harmony with others begins with harmony with oneself. For it is true, as Shakespeare said, there are great benefits available to those who comply with his admonition, "To thine own self be true, and it must follow, as the night the day, thou cannot then be false to any man."

4. Freedom from Fear

No man who is held captive by fear is rich nor is he free. Fear is a harbinger of evil, an insult to the Creator who provided man with the means of rejecting all things whatsoever which are not desired by giving him complete control over his mind power. Before grading yourself on freedom from fear, be sure to probe deeply into your soul and make certain that not one of the seven basic fears is hiding within you. And remember, when these seven basic fears have been transmuted into faith, you will have arrived at the point in your life where you can take possession of your own mind, *and through that possession acquire all your desire in life, as well as reject all you do not desire.* Without this Freedom From Fear, the other eleven riches of life may be useless.

In a subsequent chapter you will find the formula with which you can conquer the fear of ill health and physical pain.

Apply the formula and conquer this fear, then follow through and conquer the other six basic fears with the same formula.

5. The Hope of Future Achievement

Hope is the forerunner of the greatest of all states of mind—faith! Hope sustains one in times of emergency when without it fear would take over. Hope is the basic of the most profound form of happiness, which comes from the expectancy of success in some as yet unattained plan or purpose. Poor indeed is the person who cannot look toward the future with the hope he will become the person he would like to be, or attain the position he would like to hold in life, or attain the objective he has failed to acquire in the past. Hope keeps the soul of man alert and active in his behalf, *and clears the line of communication by which Faith connects one with Infinite Intelligence*. Hope is a right royal person and the Divine Decorator of the other eleven riches of life.

6. The Capacity for Faith

Faith is the means of communication between the conscious mind of man and the great universal reservoir of Infinite Intelligence. It is the fertile soil of the garden spot of the human mind wherein may be produced all of the riches of life. It is the "eternal elixir" which gives creative power and action to the impulses of thought. It is the "élan vital" of the soul, and it is without limitations. Faith is the spiritual quality which when mixed with prayer gives one direct and immediate connection with Infinite Intelligence. Faith is the power which transmutes the ordinary energies of thought into their spiritual equivalent, and it is the only means by which Infinite Intelligence may be appropriated to the uses of man.

7. Willingness to Share One's Blessings

He who has not learned the blessed art of sharing his blessings with others has not found the true path to enduring happiness, for happiness comes mainly from sharing oneself and one's blessings. Let it be remembered that the space one occupies in the hearts of others is determined precisely by the service he renders through some form of sharing. Let it be also remembered that all riches may be embellished and multiplied by the simple process of sharing them where they may serve others. Neglect or refusal to share one's blessings is a sure way to cut the line of communication between a man and his soul. A great philosopher said: "*The greatest among you is he who becomes the servant of all.*" Another great philosopher said: "Help thy brother's boat across and lo thine own hath reached the shore." And still another great philosopher said: "Whatsoever you do to or for another you do to or for yourself."

8. A Labor of Love

There can be no richer man than he who has found that a labor of love is the highest form of expression of human desires. Labor is the liaison between the demand and the supply of all human needs, the forerunner of all human progress, the medium by which the imagination of man is given wings of action. And all labor of love is sanctified because it brings the joy of self-expression to him who performs it. Do the thing you like best, and your life will be thereby enriched, your soul will be embellished, and you will be an inspiration for hope, faith, and encouragement to all with whom you come into contact. Engagement in a labor of love is the greatest of all cures for melancholy, frustration, and fear. And it is a builder of physical health without equal.

9. An Open Mind On All Subjects

Tolerance, which is among the higher attributes of culture, is expressed only by the person who holds an open mind on all subjects, toward all people, at all times. And only the person who maintains an open mind becomes truly educated and is thus prepared to embrace and use the twelve great riches of life. A closed mind atrophies and cuts off the line of communication between an individual and Infinite Intelligence. An open mind keeps the individual eternally in the process of education and the acquisition of knowledge with which he may take possession of his mind and direct it to the attainment of any desired purpose.

10. Self-Discipline

The person who is not the master of himself may never become the master of anything outside of himself. He who is the master of self may become the master of his own earthly destiny, the "Master of his Fate, the Captain of his Soul." And the highest form of self-discipline consists in the expression of humility of the heart when one has attained great riches or has been blessed with widespread recognition for services rendered.

Self-discipline is the only means by which one may take full and complete possession of his own mind and direct it to the attainment of whatsoever ends he may desire.

11. The Capacity To Understand People

The person who is rich in understanding of people recognize that all people are fundamentally alike in that they have evolved from the same stem: that all human activities, good or bad, are inspired by one or more of the nine basic motives of life, viz:

1. The emotion of LOVE
2. The emotion of SEX
3. The desire for MATERIAL GAIN
4. The desire for SELF-PRESERVATION
5. The desire for FREEDOM OF BODY AND MIND
6. The desire for RECOGNITION AND SELF-EXPRESSION
7. The desire for PERPETUATION OF LIFE AFTER DEATH
8. The emotion of ANGER
9. The emotion of FEAR (See the seven basic fears)

And the man who would understand others must first understand himself, for the motives which inspire him to action are, in the main, the same motives which would inspire others to action under the same conditions.

The capacity to understand others is the basis of all friendships; it is the basis of all harmony and cooperation among people, and the fundamental of greatest importance in all forms of leadership which call for friendly cooperation. And some believe it is an approach of major importance in the understanding of the overall plan of the universe and the Creator thereof.

Know yourself, and you will be well on the road to understanding others.

12. Economic Security (Money)

The last, but not the least of importance, is the tangible portion of the twelve great riches—money, or the knowledge with which to ensure one's economic security. Economic security is not attained by the possession of money alone. It is attained by the service one renders, for useful service may be converted into all forms of human needs, with or without the use of money.

Henry Ford attained economic security, not necessarily because he accumulated a vast fortune in money, but for the better reason that he provided profitable employment for millions of men and women, as well as dependable automobile transportation for still greater numbers of people.

Men and women who master and apply the Science of Success because he believed that the know-how of the accumulation of money should be known to everyone. During the latter portion of his life Andrew Carnegie gave away most of his vast fortune of almost a billion dollars, but in a conversation with me shortly before he died, he said:

> *I have given most of my fortune back to the people from*
> *whence it was accumulated, but the money I have given*
> *away is infinitesimally small in comparison with the riches I*
> *am leaving to the people in the "know how" of success, which*
> *I have entrusted to you for delivery to the world.*

You now have an understanding of the antithesis of poverty in the twelve great riches of life. And it should be encouraging to observe that the first eleven of these riches are within the reach of all who will embrace them, and those who do embrace and use them will easily attract the twelfth of the riches, money.

Here, then, is the means by which poverty may be transmuted into riches, including the twelve of the great riches of life.

Embrace the twelve great riches, apply them in your daily life, and you will become a success, for success is nothing more nor less than the attainment of these twelve blessings.

"Every adversity, every unpleasant experience,
every failure, carries with it the seed of an
equivalent or greater benefit."

—*Succeed and Grow Rich Through Persuasion*

The Fifth
Miracle of Life

FAILURE MAY BE A BLESSING

FAILURE often becomes a blessing in disguise, because it turns people back from contemplated purposes which had they been carried out would have meant embarrassment or even total destruction. Failure often opens new doors of opportunity and provides one with useful knowledge of the realities of life, by the trial-and-error method. Failure often reveals the methods which will not work and cures vain people of their conceit.

Failure of the British armies under Lord Cornwallis in 1781 not only gave the American colonies their freedom, but probably saved the British Empire from total destruction in World Wars I and II.

The economic failure of the South, due to the end of slavery in the war between the states eventually yielded the seed of an equivalent benefit in more ways than one, viz:

1. People begin depending upon themselves, and thereby they developed personal initiative.
2. Women of the South became more independent by taking their places alongside of men in business and in the professions.
3. And at long last, American industry is rapidly moving southward, where labor, raw materials, fuel, and weather conditions are more favorable, thanks to the personal initiative of southerners, who stopped hating the Yankees and started selling the South to northern industry.

In due time, the South may become the industrial center of the United States.

Dr. Alexander Graham Bell spent years of research looking for the means of creating a mechanical hearing aid for his hard-of-hearing wife. In his original purpose he failed, but the research yielded the secret of the long-distance telephone.

When radio first began to be popular about 1920, the Victor Talking Machine Company became frightened because it appeared that radio would ruin the talking machine business. The chief engineer of the Victor Talking Machine Company discovered, *in the principle of radio itself*, the means by which better recordings could be made, and from that discovery was born a demand for talking machines such as the company never would have known without this discovery.

Thomas A. Edison's first major failure came when his teacher sent him home from school, after only three months of schooling, with a note to his parents stating that the lad had an "addled" mind and could not take *education*. This so shocked Edison that he began acquiring an education in that great school known as the university of hard knocks and through that schooling became the greatest inventor of all times.

Also, Edison's hard of hearing might have been considered by some people as a failure of major proportions, but Edison adapted himself to it in such a way that he developed the power to hear "from within," through his sixth sense, and this perhaps was a strong factor in his ability to uncover so many of Nature's secrets in his business of inventing.

The loss of my mother, who died when I was a very young lad, would have been considered by some people as a handicap of major proportions, but it turned out differently. I was compensated for the loss of my mother with a stepmother whose influence upon me was so profound that she inspired me to engage in a calling which has benefited millions of people now living and may benefit still other millions not yet born.

I felt that I had met with a major failure when a great uncle who was a multimillionaire, after whom I was named, died and left no portion of his fortune to me. I later had reason to be thankful that I was left out of the will. This made it necessary for me to master poverty on my own account, through my own initiative, *and in doing so I learned the way to teach millions of others how to master poverty.*

Analyze failure under whatsoever circumstances you choose, and you will discover the profound truth that every failure brings with it the seed of an equivalent benefit. This does not mean that failure brings with it the full ripened fruit of an equivalent benefit, but only the seed which must be discovered, imagination and definiteness of purpose.

Most men would consider the loss of the use of their legs a failure of major proportions, but Franklin D. Roosevelt so related himself to such a loss that it gave him a determined spirit to get along with artificial braces, and he seemed to have done very well by himself without the use of his leg. His *mental attitude* toward his affliction was such that he reduced his handicap to a minimum of inconvenience.

The failure of Abraham Lincoln in storekeeping, surveying, soldiering, and the practice of law, turned his talents in a direction which prepared him to become the greatest president the United States ever has known.

More than twenty major failures which I experienced during the early part of my career changed my path and guided me eventually to give the world its first practical philosophy of personal achievement.

Clarence Saunders's failure as a store clerk yielded him an idea from which he made a profit of four million dollars in four years. That idea was the Piggly-Wiggly system of self-help grocery stores, which marked the beginning of the self-help store system now in operation on a widespread scale throughout the country.

Failure in physical health often diverts attention of the individual from his physical body to his brain; introduces him to the real "boss" of the physical body, the mind; and opens wide the horizons of opportunity which he never would have known without the failure.

Milo C. Jones of Fort Atkinson, Wisconsin, made a bare living from his farm until he was stricken by double paralysis and suffered total loss of the use of his body. Then he made a discovery which only such an affliction could have uncovered for him. He discovered that he had a mind and its possibilities of achievement were limited only by his desire and demands upon it, even without the use of his physical body. Through the aid of his mind he conceived the idea of making sausage from young hogs, named his product "Little Pig Sausage," and lived to become a multimillionaire.

The fact that Mr. Jones did not discover his fabulous source of riches while he had the full use of his physical body is something which provides food for profound thought. The great law of change had to throw Milo C. Jones flat on his back and break up his old habits, by which he earned his living with his hands, in order to introduce him to his brain power which he discovered to be infinitely greater than his brawn power.

Verily, nature never permits an individual to be deprived of any of his inborn rights and blessings without providing him with the potential of an equivalent benefit in some other form, as in the case of Milo C. Jones.

Failure is a blessing or a curse, depending upon the individual's reaction to it. If one looks upon failure as a sort of judge from the hand of destiny, which signals him to move in another direction, and if he acts upon that signal, the experience is practically sure to become a blessing. If he accepts failure as an indication of his weakness and broods over it until it produces an inferiority complex, then it is a curse. *The nature of the reaction* tells the story, and this is under the exclusive control of the individual always.

No one has complete immunity against failure, and everyone meets with failure many times during a lifetime, but everyone also has the privilege and the means by which he can react to failure in any manner he pleases.

Circumstances over which one has no control may, and they sometimes do, result in failure, but there are no circumstances which can prevent one from reacting to failure in a manner best suited for his benefit. Failure is an accurate measuring device by which an individual may determine his weaknesses, and it provides, therefore, an opportunity for correcting them. In this sense failure always is a blessing.

Failure usually affects people in one or the other of two ways: it serves only as a challenge to greater effort or it subdues and discourages one from trying again. The majority of people give up hope and quit at the first sign of failure, even before it overtakes them. And a large percentage of people quit when they are overtaken by a single failure. The potential leader never is subdued by failure, but always is inspired to greater effort by it. Watch your failures and you will learn whether you have potentialities for leadership. Your personal reaction will give you a dependable cue.

If you can keep on trying after three failures in a given undertaking, you may consider yourself a "suspect" as a potential leader in your chosen occupation. *If you can keep on trying after a dozen failures, the seed of a genius is germinating within your soul.* Give it the sunshine of hope and faith, and watch it grow into great personal achievements.

It appears that Nature often knocks individuals down with adversities in order to learn who among them *will get up and make another fight*! Those who make the grade are chosen as people of destiny, to serve as leaders in work of great importance to mankind.

The next time you meet with failure, if you will remember that every failure, and every adversity, carries with it the seed of an equivalent benefit, and start where you stand to recognize that seed and begin to germinate it through action, you may discover that *there never is any such reality as failure until one accepts it as such*!

It would have been most natural and logical for Milo C. Jones to have accepted his affliction as a knockout blow from which he never could recover, and no one would have blamed him if he had done so, but he reacted to his handicap in a positive manner, which yielded him a better working relationship with the power of his mind. His *reaction* was the important part of the experience, because it paid off in terms of financial riches such as he had never dreamed of acquiring.

Most so-called failures are only temporary defeats which can be converted into assets of a priceless nature if one takes a positive mental attitude toward them.

From birth until death, life poses a constant challenge to people to master failure without going down for the count, and rewards with bountiful opulence and great personal powers those who successfully meet the challenge.

The world generously forgives one for his mistakes and temporary defeats, provided always that he accepts them as such and keeps on trying, *but there is no forgiveness for the sin of quitting when the going is hard*! Life's motto is: "A WINNER NEVER QUITS AND A QUITTER NEVER WINS!"

Japan's failure in World War II was her greatest victory, since that failure broke the vicious yoke of satisfaction by which the Japanese people had been bound and gave them their first taste of democracy and an opportunity to take their place in the family of civilized peoples on an equality with all others.

In all human endeavors Nature seems to favor the "fool" who did not know he could fail, but who went ahead and did the "impossible" before he discovered it couldn't be done.

Henry J. Kaiser had never built seaworthy ships, but the emergency of World War II called for more ships than the established shipbuilding sources could supply. So Kaiser began building ships with such faith and enthusiasm that he literally "ran rings" around the older and more experienced men in that business, *with an all-time high in production and an all-time low in cost*!

The man who says, "It can't be done," usually winds up under the feet of the man who is busy doing it, *the man who succeeds because he has thrown himself in the path of the laws of the universe and adapted himself to their habits* and thereby insured himself against failure. The man who says, "It can't be done," has never studied Nature's laws.

An old miner spent thirty years in search of precious metals, only to meet with disappointment and despair until he was overtaken by the misfortune of having his trusty mule break its leg in a gopher hole. The mule had to be shot. While digging a hole in which to bury the animal the miner struck the richest copper deposit in the entire world!

Destiny often selects dramatic ways in which to reward people for stick-to-itiveness and the will to keep on trying in the face of defeat.

In this world of practical realism, one must constantly remind himself that *our only limitations are those which we set up in our own minds or permit others* to establish for us. Recognition of this great truth makes all so-called "failures" look pretty tame!

Henceforth and forever remember that no experience can be classified as a failure unless and until it has been accepted as such! Remember, also, that only the person who meets with a given experience has the right to call it a failure, or by some other name, and that the verdict of all others is ruled out.

Fifty-Four Major Causes of Failure

1. The habit of drifting with circumstances, without definite aims or purposes.
2. Unfavorable physical heredity at birth.
3. Meddlesome curiosity in connection with other people's affairs.
4. Lack of a definite major purpose as a life goal.
5. Inadequate schooling.
6. Lack of self-discipline, which generally manifests itself through excesses in eating, drinking, and sex indulgence, and indifference toward opportunities for self-advancement.
7. Lack of ambition to aim above mediocrity.
8. Ill health, generally due to wrong thinking, improper diet, and lack of physical exercise. (Keep in mind, however, that some people, such as Helen Keller, have made themselves of great service to others despite incurable ailments.)
9. Unfavorable environmental influences during childhood. It has been said that the major fundamentals of character have been well formed in the individual by the time he is seven years of age.
10. Lack of persistence in carrying through to a finish that which one starts.
11. A negative mental attitude as a fixation of habit.
12. Lack of control over the emotions of the heart.

13. Desire for something for nothing, usually expressed in the habit of gambling.

14. Failure to reach decisions promptly and definitely and to stand by them after they have been made.

15. One or more of the seven basic fears.

16. Wrong selection of a mate in marriage.

17. Overcaution in business and professional relationships.

18. Lack of all forms of caution.

19. Wrong choice of associates in business or professional pursuits.

20. Wrong selection of a vocation, or total neglect to make a choice.

21. Lack of concentration of effort on the task at hand at a given time.

22. Habit of indiscriminate spending, without a budget control over income and expenditures.

23. Failure to budget and use TIME to best advantage.

24. Lack of *controlled* enthusiasm.

25. Intolerance; a closed mind based particularly on ignorance or prejudice in connection with religious, political, and economic subjects.

26. Failure to cooperate with others in a spirit of harmony.

27. The possession of power or wealth not based on merit or not earned.

28. Lack of the spirit of loyalty to whom loyalty is due.

29. Egotism of forming opinion and building plans without basing them on firsthand knowledge of the necessary facts.

30. Habit of forming opinions and building plans without basing plans without basing them on firsthand knowledge of the necessary facts.

31. Lack of vision and imagination sufficient to recognize favorable opportunities.

32. Unwillingness to go the extra mile in rendering service.

33. The desire for revenge for real or imaginary injuries by others.

34. The habit of conversing in terms of vulgarity or profanity.

35. The habit of indulging in negative gossip about the affairs of other people.

36. Unsocial attitude toward one's constituted authorities of government.

37. Unbelief in the existence of Infinite Intelligence.

38. Lack of knowledge of how to engage in prayer so as to bring positive results.

39. Failure to benefit by the counsel of others whose experience one often needs.

40. Carelessness in the payment of personal debts.

41. The habit of lying or unduly modifying the truth.

42. The habit of offering criticism where it has not been invited.

43. Overextension in connection with the incurring of indebtedness.

44. Greed for material possessions one does not need.

45. Lack of self-confidence of adequate proportions for the fulfillment of one's chosen objective.

46. Alcoholism or narcotics.

47. Overindulgence in smoking.

48. The habit (of laymen) of serving as their own lawyers in connection with contracts and legal matters.
49. The habit of endorsing other people's notes when the risk is not justified.
50. The habit of procrastination; putting off until tomorrow that which should have been attended to the day before yesterday.
51. The habit of running away from unpleasant circumstances instead of mastering them.
52. The habit of talking too much and listening too little. One never learns anything while talking, but always is in the way of learning by listening when others talk.
53. The habit of accepting favors from others without reciprocating.
54. Intentional dishonesty in business and professional relations.

Check yourself carefully by these fifty-four causes of failure, and should the self-examination reveal that you can check OK after each of the causes, it is not likely you will ever be overcome by failure. Moreover, if you can check yourself OK after each of these causes of failure, you need not worry over dental or surgical operations, for you have everything under control.

After you make your own rating, however, it may be both interesting and helpful if you have some other person rate you on each of these causes of failure—someone who knows you quite well and has the courage to let you look at yourself through his or her eyes.

"To be a star, you must shine your own light, follow your own path, and don't worry about darkness, for that is when the stars shine brightest."

—*Think and Grow Rich*

The Sixth
Miracle of Life

SORROW, THE PATH TO THE SOUL

SORROW never is invited by individuals, but it is one of the more effective devices of Nature through which human beings are conditioned to become humble and cooperative in human relationships.

When a person who has known great sorrow is tempted to criticize or condemn those with whom he may not agree or those who may have injured him, often he reverses the general rule in such circumstances, and instead of condemning often says, "God pity us all!" When we meet this type of person, we intuitively recognize that we are in the presence of royalty!

Sorrow is medicine for the soul, without which the soul would never be recognized by many. Without the leavening influence of sorrow man would still be on the same stem with the animals on the lower plane of intelligence. Sorrow breaks down the barriers which stand between physical man and his spiritual potentialities.

Sorrow breaks up old habits and replaces them with new and better habits, a fact which suggests that sorrow is a device of Nature by which she keeps man from becoming subjugated by complacency and self-satisfaction.

Through my one and only great sorrow I discovered the path to my own soul which gave me freedom I would never have known without this experience and paved the way for the writing of this book.

Sorrow is closely akin to the emotions of love, the greatest of all the emotions, and during times of disaster sorrow brings people together in a spirit of friendship and influences man to recognize the blessings of becoming his brother's keeper.

Sorrow softens poverty and embellishes riches!

The riches which are revealed only by sorrow are so great and so varied that inventory of them is impossible. The capacity for sorrow, within itself, is evidence of one's deep spiritual qualities. Knaves never know the emotion of sorrow, for if they knew sorrow they would not be knaves.

Sorrow forces man to take introspective inventory of himself, wherein he may discover the cure for all his ills and disappointments. And it introduces one to the benefits of meditation and silence, during which unseen forces may bring aid and comfort sufficient unto one's needs at a given time or experience.

When a man comes to himself and discovers the stupendous powers within his command, the revelation usually is the result of some experience of great sorrow: the loss of a loved one, failure in business, or some physical affliction beyond his control. There are certain necessary refinements of body and mind which Nature seems to bring about solely by the device of sorrow, such as the elimination of selfishness, arrogance, vanity, and self-love.

Sorrow, like failure, may be a blessing or a curse, according to one's reaction to it. If it is accepted as a necessary disciplinary force, without resentment, it may become a great blessing. If it is resented, and one sees no benefits growing out of it, then it may become a curse. The choice is entirely in the mind of the individual.

Sometimes sorrow becomes self-pity, and as such it serves only to weaken the one who so embraces it. Sorrow is beneficial only when it is experienced as an emotional feeling of sympathy for others or accepted by the individual as a welcome medium of discipline.

One never is in closer contact with Infinite Intelligence than in times of deep sorrow. It is in times of sorrow that prayer is most effective, and often the prayer brings positive results instantly. Sorrow has revealed to the world geniuses who never would have been recognized except for its deep soul-searching effects. Abraham Lincoln's sorrow over the only woman he ever truly loved, Anne Rutledge, revealed to the world his great soul and gave him to America as our greatest leader in times of our direst need.

Frustration, brought about by unrequited love, often brings one to a turning-point in life at which sorrow makes its appearance, and serves as a guide to great achievements or a stumbling block which may bring total destruction, according to the way the individual relates himself to it. Here, again, the choice is entirely with the individual. Not even the Creator will abrogate one's privilege of controlling his own mind and directing it to whatever ends he may choose, *and no other power can cancel this privilege except by consent of the individual.*

Sorrow may become a mighty power for good when it is transmuted into some sort of constructive action or personal reformation. Sorrow has been known to cure one of the diseases of alcoholism after everything else had failed. And it is a recognized cure for most of the sins of man. Someone has said, "When sorrow fails, the Devil takes over."

In times of sorrow people throw off all devices of pretense and reveal themselves as they are, for sorrow is an hour for open confession of both the humble and the proud. Without the emotion of sorrow man would be an animal as ferocious as the wildest tiger, but infinitely more dangerous because of his superior intelligence.

In lifting man to the highest plane of intelligence the Creator wisely refined that intelligence with a capacity for sorrow to ensure man's moderation in the use of his superiority. Sadists and master criminals usually are individuals of great intelligence but who lack the capacity for sorrow.

A man without the capacity for sorrow is the nearest thing known as a Devil in the *flesh*.

If you should ever feel that your sorrows are greater than you can bear, remember you are at a crossroads of life, with four directions from which to choose, one of which may lead you to peace of mind which you would never have found in any other direction or by any other means. Remember too that the person who has never felt the hand of sorrow has never really lived, for sorrow is the Master-Key to the gateway of one's soul, the port of entrance to Infinite Intelligence.

Sorrow is a stopgap, a sort of safety valve, which protects those who refuse to heed the guidance of their faculty of reason. Sorrow is a tonic to great souls a bludgeon to the weak and the undisciplined.

I graduated in the University of Sorrow at the age of fifty. From birth until I reached the age of fifty, I had met with about every sort of sorrow one can experience, and somehow I had triumphed over all these. All my rivers of sorrow had been crossed except one which proved to be the last and the greatest of them all. This was a new sort of sorrow against which I had not built a wall of immunity, and it involved the most profound and yet the most dangerous of the emotions, the emotion of love.

I had wandered into the Garden of Love by a path which proved to be a labyrinth over which I found it difficult to backtrack. I had seen hundreds of my students make this same mistake, and always I had felt something only slightly less than contempt for them because of their weakness. Now the shoe was on my foot and it pinched tightly.

At long last I knew, at first hand, the sorrow of unrequited love, and I knew also that I had to find a way to transmute this experience into some form of constructive action. With this experience, as with all previous similar experiences, I began the transmutation by setting for myself a work task which left me no time for grieving.

By some strange move of the Hand of Fate, I was guided to the little town of Clinton, South Carolina, where I settled down to lick my heart wounds and rewrite the *Science of Success*, a task which required over a year. In the apartment where I lived alone was an oil painting of a beautiful forest through which flowed a wide river that faded from sight at a sharp bend which changed the river's course.

Night after night I sat in front of that painting, waiting and watching for the Ship of Hope to sail around the bend, but the ship never came, and the days turned into weeks and the weeks into months which found me alone with myself. I had always managed to escape from every other unpleasant circumstance of my life, but here I was, seemingly inseparably imprisoned with myself, and the boredom seemed greater than I could endure.

I was destined to learn from this experience one of the greatest lessons of my meteoric career, namely, that man is not complete without the companionship of the woman of his choice. I could have learned the lesson in no other way.

One evening, after I had been living alone with myself for a year, I was dressing for a dinner engagement and the lights in my apartment were low. I happened to glance at the painting on the wall, and by some strange phenomenon due to the faint light showing on the picture, I saw a perfect picture of a ship coming around the bend. "My Ship of Hope at last," I exclaimed.

As I sat across the table from my dinner guest that evening I made another discovery which clearly revealed to me why I had been guided to the little town of Clinton, for there in front of me sat my future wife, the one for whom I had been searching hither and yon, not knowing that she lived almost next door to me.

So out of my greatest sorrow the eternal law of compensation yielded me the greatest of all my riches, a wife perfectly suited in every way to walk arm in arm with me down through the afternoon of life, while we work together putting on the finishing touches of a career through which sorrow has been transmuted into a philosophy destined to benefit millions of people, some of them as yet unborn.

But the payoff never would have come, the *Science of Success* philosophy never would have been organized, had I not learned the blessed art of transmuting unpleasant circumstances into constructive action.

Remember this word "transmute" when you sit in a dentist's chair again, and keep your mind so busily engaged in thinking of something constructive that no time will be left for you to feel physical pain. And when sorrow overtakes you, follow the same plan by turning your thoughts toward the attainment of some as yet unattained purpose; keep it so busy thinking of ways and means of attaining that purpose that no time will be left for self-pity. Do this and you will discover a hidden asset you did not know you possessed: an asset worth more than a king's ransom. *You will discover that you are the master of yourself!*

I know something of the effects of sorrow because I was born in the midst of oceans of it (and I was born to an inheritance of poverty as well). The home in which I was born was a one-room log cabin located in the mountains of southwest Virginia, and our total assets at the time of my birth consisted of one horse, one cow, one bed, and a bake-oven in which my mother baked corn bread.

It is a little cause for wonder, therefore, that I came into this world screaming with fright, for I was born in an environment but little in advance of that of the caveman during precivilization days.

Theoretically, I had not the ghost of a chance of ever becoming a free man and less of a chance of ever becoming of service to my fellow men throughout the world. My parents were poor and they were illiterate. Our neighbors were poor and also illiterate. The only asset of value which I inherited at birth was a sound physical body and a healthy bloodstream.

In addition to all these handicaps under which I was born, my father was a religious fanatic and I had to protect myself from this influence. Once he beat me until I was unconscious because I went fishing on Sunday instead of going to church and listening to five old fogies, each of whom preached for an hour on the sins of man, of which I am sure they knew nothing. All of them talked glibly about "sin" but not one of them got around to telling what was sin.

From this brief description of my background, you may wonder why I was chosen to give the world its first and only practical philosophy of personal success. I have often wondered about that myself! But the philosopher tells us that, "God moves in a mysterious way, His wonders to perform."

Out of the sorrows of my childhood came a passionate desire to lessen the sorrows of others, a desire so strong and enduring that it carried me through more than twenty years of profitless research into the causes of success and failure. Perhaps the sorrows of my youth were sent my way on purpose, in order that I might be inspired to render the world useful service.

When I say "profitless research" I mean, of course, profitless in monetary compensation while the research was being carried on. As to the ultimate compensation which this research yielded me, I can say sincerely I doubt that any other author ever had as much help or as favorable an opportunity to carry on any sort of literacy work as I had during those twenty years, while the *Science of Success* was being organized. At long last those "profitless" years helped me project my influence, for good, into the lives of millions of people and yielded to me personally more than any share of the Twelve Great Riches, *which represent all there is in personal success on this earthly plane.*

If I could go back and live my life over again, would I avoid those sorrows of my youth? No, definitely I would not, for it was those experiences which tempered my body and mind and refined my soul for a task in life which is without equal as to the extent and quality of the benefits my work has provided for others who are struggling to find their way through the Black Forest of the Jungle of Life.

Get the full significance of the thought I am here trying to convey, and you will understand why I stated that this volume would be something profoundly greater than the mere instructions on how to master the fear of dentistry or surgical operations. If I do my work as I have hoped I might do it in the writing of this volume, *it will introduce the reader to a source of power with which all unpleasant circumstances can be transmuted into helpful services*; a source of power which operates through that "other self" which one does not see when looking into a mirror.

Once you learn to properly evaluate sorrow, you will recognize its benefits whenever they appear, and you will understand it is one of the more essential devices of Nature *with which she separates man from his animalistic background.* Animals on all planes of development lower than that of man never feel the beneficent emotion of sorrow, with the exception of the dog whose long partnership with man has made the dog something closely akin to, but slightly less than, a human being.

If you have a great capacity for sorrow, you have also a great potential capacity for genius, provided you relate yourself to sorrow as a welcome source of discipline and not as a medium of self-pity.

As we continue on our trip through the Valley of the Great Miracles you will observe that each of them is definitely embellished with spiritual potentialities of great benefit to those who correctly interpret them. And you will observe, also, *that peace of mind is available only to those who properly interpret and relate themselves to the laws of Nature.* If you miss this point, you will have missed the major purpose which prompted the writing of this book!

Sorrow is the great universal denominator which serves to compose the circumstances of a community, or a family, when misfortune strikes. I have known sorrow to bring together estranged husbands and wives who would have yielded to no other influence, and I have seen sorrow wipe out mountain feuds which had existed for generations.

The emotion of sorrow, like the emotion of love, refines the souls of those who experience it, and gives them courage and faith to meet the trials and tribulations of struggle in a world of confusion and chaos, *provided always that sorrow is accepted as a benefit and not as a curse.* Resentment of sorrow develops stomach ulcers, high blood pressure, and general unfriendliness from other people.

Remember every sorrow brings with it the seed of an equivalent joy! Look for that seed, germinate it, and reap the benefit of the joy. When you can do this, you will no longer permit yourself to be annoyed by so trivial a matter as dental or surgical operations, even if they are major operations. Instead of coddling yourself when you meet with sorrow, look around until you find someone with a greater sorrow than yours and help him or her to master it. And lo! *Your own sorrow will have been transmuted into medicine for your body and your soul*—the sort of medicine with which you may cure many other types of unpleasant experiences.

"Sometimes it appears there is a hidden guide whose duty is to test people through all sorts of discouraging experiences. Those who pick themselves up after defeat and keep on trying arrive. . . . The hidden guide lets no one enjoy great achievement without passing the persistence test. Those who can't take it simply do not make the grade. . . ."

—Think and Grow Rich

The Seventh Miracle of Life

OUR UNSEEN GUIDES

OUR UNSEEN GUIDES, whose existence can be proved only by those who have recognized them and accepted the services, remain at our service from the time of our birth until death. These invisible talismans remain with us while we are awake and watch over us while we sleep, although most people go through life without recognizing their existence.

It is not my purpose to give a long dissertation as evidence of the existence of unseen guides who aid human beings, but merely to bring them to the attention of my fellow wayfarers who are willing to accept whatever sources of aid they can find in their search for a way of life which satisfies one's needs and leads to peace of mind.

Had it not been for the aid I received from my friendly unseen guides, I never could have given the world the Science of Success which now aids millions of people to recognize and make practical use of their *inner sources of power*.

Eight of my unseen guides have been recognized and named, each with a name appropriate to the nature of the service it renders. They are here described in detail, with an explanation as to the scope and nature of the service each renders and how that service is rendered, but one should keep in mind the fact that the Eight Guiding Princes are the product of my own imagination, and they may be duplicated by anyone who chooses to engage them.

I treat my Eight Guiding Princes as though they were real people whose entire services are at my command throughout my life. I give them orders and thank them for their services just as I would do if they were people. And they react to my requests as though they were real people.

A description of the Eight Guiding Princes together with an explanation of the service each performs, now follows.

THE EIGHT GUIDING PRINCES

1. PRINCE OF FINANCIAL PROSPERITY

The sole responsibility of this invisible guide is to keep me adequately supplied with every material thing which I desire or need to maintain the style of living which I have adopted. Money worries which destroy the peace of mind of so many people throughout their lives is something I never experience. When I need money, it is always available in whatever amounts I may require, *but money is neither expected nor obtained without my giving something of equal value in return*, usually some form of service rendered for the benefit of others.

2. PRINCE OF SOUND PHYSICAL HEALTH

The sole responsibility of this invisible guide is that of keeping my physical body in perfect order at all times, including the conditioning of the body for any adjustments which have to be made, such as that of preparation for dentistry. Before this Prince took over, I was subject to headaches, constipation, and at times physical exhaustion, all of which have been corrected. The Prince of Sound Physical Health keeps all the vital organs of my body alert and functioning at all times, keeps the billions of individual cells of my body properly charged with bodily resistance, *and provides adequate immunity against all contagious diseases.*

Let it be remembered, however, that I cooperate with the Prince of Sound Physical Health by sensible living habits, such as proper eating, the right amount of sleep, *and habits which balance my work with an equal amount of play.* But particularly, *I keep my mind occupied with positive, constructive thinking,* and never permit it to engage in any form of fear, superstition, or hypochondria. And last, with every morsel of food and every drop of liquid which goes into my mouth *I add a generous mixture of worship* through which I express thanks to my invisible guide, the Prince of Sound Physical Health, for maintenance of perfect health throughout my body. I most enjoy a peaceful calmness throughout my life, in all my activities and experiences, but especially do I make it a business to eat my food in an atmosphere of joyous serenity. We have no set hour for family discipline in our home, but if we did have such an hour, *it would not be at mealtime,* as is the case in many homes. Every thought one expresses while eating becomes a part of the energy which goes into the food and enters the bloodstream, and that thought makes its way to the brain where it blesses or curses one according to whether the thought is positive or negative. Evidence of this truth may be found in the case of the mother who nurses her child at her breast. If she becomes worried or negative minded for any reason while the child is nursing, her state of mind will poison her milk and give the child indigestion or colic. And of course it is well known to doctors that most stomach ulcers are due mainly to worry and negative thinking.

It is obvious, therefore, that the Prince of Sound Physical Health must have a considerable amount of intelligent cooperation in order to keep the physical body operating efficiently and normally. This is the price one must pay for good health.

3. PRINCE OF PEACE OF MIND

The sole responsibility of this invisible guide is to keep the mind free from disturbing influences such as fear, superstition, greed, envy, hatred, and covetousness. The work of the Prince of Peace of Mind is closely related to that of the prince of sound physical health. Through the work of this invisible guide one may shut off all thoughts of unpleasant circumstances of the past, and all thoughts of unpleasant experiences contemplated for the future, such as that of surgical operations or dentistry.

The Prince of Peace of Mind keeps the mind so fully occupied with subjects of one's choosing that there is no space left in it for voluntary, stray thoughts of a negative nature. *To these the doors to the mind are tightly closed!* This invisible guide throws a wall of protection around one which keeps out everything which could lead to worry, fear, or anxiety of any nature, except only those circumstances which have a legitimate right to consideration in connection with one's obligations to others, and these are so modified that they are easily managed.

There always are human relations which may be temporarily unpleasant, which one must recognize and deal with, such as the details of management of a business, a profession, or a job, or the family budget, and there always are unpleasant emergencies one must meet with, such as the death of friends and loved ones. To all of these the Prince of Peace of Mind helps the individual to relate himself *without being thrown off of mental balance*.

4. PRINCE OF HOPE and 5. PRINCE OF FAITH (Operating as Twins)

The sole responsibility of these invisible guides is that of keeping the gateway to Infinite Intelligence open to me at all times, under all circumstances. These twins keep me from handicapping myself with unnecessary limitations in connection with my life work, and they help me so organize my plans that *they conform to the laws of Nature and the rights of my fellow men*. They help me, also, see my plans a completed reality, *even before I begin putting them into operation*, and they turn me back from undertaking any plan or purpose if it were carried out, which might be of ultimate harm to me or to others.

The Princes of Hope and Faith keep me in constant touch with the spiritual forces which operate through me, and they guide me toward objectives which benefit everyone with whom I come into contact, either in person or by my written works. Here, then, is the explanation as to why the readers of my books are so universally successful in the planning and the living of their lives.

These Princes of Hope and Faith keep me charged with enthusiasm sufficient to insure me against procrastination. They keep my imagination alert and active in planning the work to which I devote my entire life. They help me find joy and happiness in everything I do. And they help me interpret the evils of the world without embracing them or being injured by them. They help me walk with all men, both the saints and the sinners, *and still remain the master of my own fate, the captain of my own soul*! They keep my ego alert and active, yet humble and grateful. And lastly, they help me ride the waves of chaos and confusion in a world which is undergoing rapid changes in human relations, *without giving up or neglecting my own inalienable privilege of controlling and directing my own mind to whatsoever ends I may choose.*

With Hope and Faith as my constant guides I meet successfully the resistance and the unpleasant experiences of life by transmuting them into positive forces, through which I carry my aims and purposes to conclusion. With the aid of these twin guides everything which comes to my mill of life is made into the grist of opportunity.

6. PRINCE OF LOVE and 7. PRINCE OF ROMANCE (Operating as Twins)

The sole responsibility of these invisible guides is to keep me youthful in both body and mind, and they do their work so well that I celebrate every birthday *by deducting a year from my age.* And the joyful result is that I feel, think, work, and play as if I were twenty years younger.

The Princes of Love and Romance make of my work a joy which knows not discouragement or fatigue, *and they stimulate my imagination to create with ease the patterns of all things I desire to accomplish.*

These invisible guides help me live again the loves and the fantasies of the days which have flown, and they bring back memories of past experiences which have served to introduce me to my "other self"—that self which embraces the beauties and avoids the unpleasantness of life.

Love and Romance have aided me in exchanging for wisdom, the sorrows, frustrations, and failures of the past, and they have given refinement to my soul which could have been attained by no other means. They help me recognize the objective of my earthly destiny and provide me with the means of surmounting the obstacles I must surmount to attain my destiny. They help me in making every day of my life pay off in dividends of joy which more than compensate for the necessity of struggle that each day calls for.

Love and Romance have made me flexible and adaptable to all the circumstances which affect my life, both the pleasant and the unpleasant, so that I do not forfeit the privilege of controlling and directing my mind to whatsoever ends I choose.

They provide me with a keen sense of humor with which I adjust myself favorably in all my human relations, and they help me attract the people and the circumstances which I need to make me grateful for my sojourn in life.

Love and Romance help me recognize, and germinate, and develop in growth that seed of an equivalent benefit which comes in every adversity, every frustration, every failure, and every disappointment.

Love and Romance are the sole means by which I gracefully exchange youth for the wisdom with which I write my own price tag on the business of living *and make life pay off on my own terms*. And they restrain me from, prevent me from *settling for too little*. They have taught me to pray, "Help me, oh Lord, to acquire the things which are good for me and prevent me from acquiring things I do not need."

Love and Romance are the interior decorators of the upper room in which dwells my soul! They make me grateful for the things I have, keep me from sorrowing over the things I have not. And should I indulge my Love where it is not reciprocated, Romance helps me find compensation in the joy I had *in the indulgence itself*, and to recognize that Love rebounds to the benefit of those who express it, even though it may not be reciprocated.

Love and Romance help me express pity for others where, without these guides I might express hatred and they heal quickly the wounds inflicted upon me by the injuries and injustices of others.

8. PRINCE OF OVERALL WISDOM

The responsibilities of this Prince consist in multiple services. First of all, the Prince of Overall Wisdom inspires eternal action on the part of the other seven Princes to the end that each carries out his duties to the fullest extent possible, and protects me while I sleep the same as while I am awake.

This invisible guide performs another and a very miraculous service by transmuting into benefits to me *all the failures and defeats and unpleasant circumstances I have experienced in the past* so that everything which has affected my life in the past has been converted into an asset of great value.

The Prince of Overall Wisdom gives me guidance at the crossroads of life, whenever I may be in doubt as to which road to take, and gives me the go-ahead or a stop signal in connection with all my aims, plans, and purposes.

There are other unseen Guides at my service whose names I do not know. Nor do I understand completely the full extent and nature of the service they render, except that whatever I may need to carry on my life work, or whatever I may desire *to give me continuous peace of mind*, always is at my command without effort or anxiety on my part.

These mysterious Guides first came to my attention many years ago, by interrupting my plans with failure, when I strayed away from my major mission in life, that mission being the organization and the spreading of the Science of Success. From time to time, as I gained recognition from the public in connection with my life work, I was offered what seemed to me fabulous opportunities to commercialize my talents and my experience. One of these opportunities was offered me by the late Ivy Lee, Public Relations Counselor for the Rockefeller family. Although the deal never was consummated, I did accept the offer, and that mere acceptance cost me the loss of the *Golden Rule* magazine which I had founded as a by-product of my philosophy.

After I had met with one failure after another, and each time was tempted to desert or neglect my major mission in life, I began to notice that the effects of each failure were immediately wiped out the moment I got back on track and began to carry out my mission. This happened so often that it could not be explained away as mere coincidence.

From personal experience I know there are friendly Guides available to everyone who will recognize them and accept their services. In order to avail oneself of the services of these unseen Guides two things are necessary: first, one must express gratitude for their services; second, *one must follow their guidance to the letter*. Neglect in this respect will bring sure, if not always swift, disaster. Perhaps this may explain why some people meet with disasters, the cause of which they cannot understand— disasters which they do not believe to be the results of any fault on their part.

For many years, I was so sensitive concerning the unseen Guides whose presence I had felt that I carefully avoided all references to them, in both my writings and public lectures. Then one day in a conversation with Elmer R. Gates, a distinguished scientist and inventor, I was overwhelmed with joy when I learned that he not only had discovered the presence of unseen Guides, but he had formed a working alliance with them which enabled him to perfect more inventions and procure more patents than had ever been granted to the great inventor, Thomas A. Edison.

From that day on I began to make inquiries of the hundreds of successful men who collaborated with me in the organization of the Science of Success and discovered that *each of them had received guidance from unknown sources*, although many of them were reluctant to admit this discovery. My experience with men in the upper brackets of personal achievement has been that they prefer to accredit their success to their *individual superiority*.

Thomas A. Edison, Henry Ford, Luther Burbank, Andrew Carnegie, Elmer R. Gates, and Dr. Alexander Graham Bell went to great length in their descriptions of their experiences with unseen Guides, although some of these men did not refer to these invisible sources of aid as "guides." Dr. Bell, in particular, believed the invisible source of aid was nothing but a direct contact with Infinite Intelligence, brought about by the individual's stimulation of his own mind through a burning desire for the attainment of definite objectives.

Through the guidance of unseen forces Madame Marie Curie was directed to the revelation of the secret and the source of supply of radium, although she did not know in advance where to begin looking for radium or what it would look like if she found it.

Thomas A. Edison had an interesting view as to the nature and source of the invisible forces which he used so freely in his work of research in the field of invention. He believed that all thoughts released by all people at all times are picked up and become a part of the ether, where they remain forever, just as they were released by the individuals, and that one may tune in and contact those previously released thoughts by conditioning the mind, through definiteness and clearness of purpose, to contact any desired type of thoughts which may be related to that purpose. For example, Mr. Edison discovered that when he concentrated his thoughts upon an idea he wished to perfect, he could "tune in" and pick up from the great reservoir of the boundless ether thoughts related to that idea which had been previously released by others who had thought along that same line.

Mr. Edison called attention to the fact that water runs its course, through rivers and streams; renders a great variety of services to mankind; and returns finally to the oceans from whence it came, there to become a part of the main body of water, where it is cleansed and made ready to begin its journey all over again, and that this coming and going of water, without diminishing or increasing its quantity, has a definite parallel in the energy of thought.

Edison believed that the energy with which we think is a projected portion of Infinite Intelligence. And this Intelligence becomes specialized into myriad ideas and concepts through the brain of man, and when the thoughts are released they return, like the water returns to the oceans, to the great reservoir from whence the energy came, and are there filed and classified so that all related thoughts are arranged together.

Mr. Edison definitely ruled out the belief of some who claim that the invisible Guides are departed people who once lived on earth. In this decision, I fully concur, *for I have never found the slightest evidence indicating that people who depart from the earth ever communicate with those who are living.* In fairness to those who may believe otherwise, I frankly admit that this is only my personal opinion, and that the opinion was arrived at, not by evidence, *but for the lack of evidence.*

Turning back the pages of history of civilization one cannot help but be profoundly impressed with the fact that always when people have been overtaken by some great crisis which threatened to destroy the achievements of civilization, a leader has made his appearance with the necessary *inner wisdom* to provide the means of survival and continuation of civilization.

We had evidence that adequate leadership always appears in times of great crises when the British threatened the freedom of the people of the colonies in 1776, in the person of George Washington and his little army of underfed, under clothed, undertrained, and under armed soldiers.

We had further evidence when this nation was being torn apart by inner strife, during the war between the states, in the person of the great leader Abraham Lincoln.

And we had still further evidence in World Wars I and II, when we were compelled to fight the combined forces of science, manned by barbarians who were out to destroy human rights and personal freedom all over the world.

In all such cases, there always have appeared unseen forces and circumstances, which help RIGHT to prevail over WRONG.

And every individual is born with an accompanying group of unseen Guides sufficient to supply all his or her needs, and with these guides come definite penalties for neglect to recognize and use them, also definite rewards for their recognition and use. In the main the rewards consist in the necessary wisdom to ensure the individual's success in carrying out his mission in life, whatever that may be, and to show him the way to the most priceless of all riches, *peace of mind*.

Throughout this volume I have described, though many different phrases and illustrations, the Supreme Secret of all human achievements. Those who discover this secret will receive with it the means of recognizing and bringing into their service the unseen Guides which may now lie dormant, awaiting recognition and the call to service.

The presence of these Guides, and evidence of their active service in one's behalf, will be recognized by the improvement and benefits which will begin to manifest themselves from the very day the Guides receive recognition and are given *definite instructions*.

Fantastic and impractical, does someone exclaim?

No, "miraculous" is a better word, because no one, as far as I know, has yet explained the source of these unseen Guides, or how or why they are to guide the lives of every living person. But there are thousands of people among the students of the Science of Success who know that the Guides exist because they, too, have learned the method—the Supreme Secret—by which this guidance can be acquired.

The unseen Guides are housed in that "other self" which every person possesses, that self which one does not recognize the word "impossible," nor limitations of any nature whatsoever, that self which is the master of all physical pain, sorrow, defeat, and temporary failures.

Somewhere along the way, as you read this volume, your other self may jump out from behind the lines, where you can recognize it, if you have not already done so. When that point has been reached, turn down the page and mark it for future reference, for you will have come to a profound turning point of your life.

HOW TO GIVE INSTRUCTIONS
TO YOUR OTHER SELF WHILE YOU SLEEP

The time is nearing when one may treat physical ailments, master the inferiority complexes, and condition the mind for any desired purpose while one is asleep. Moreover, it will be possible to master any desired language and acquire education on any subject while one sleeps.

The reason for this treatment while one sleeps is this: While one is awake the conscious section of the mind stands guard at the door through which the subconscious must be reached, and modifies or rejects outright all influences and instructions which one may endeavor to give the subconscious, and the conscious mind is a cynic of no small force. It seems to be more

easily influenced by fear, suspicion, and doubt than it is by positive influences. For this reason any directives one desires to give
to the subconscious can best be given when the conscious mind
is asleep and off duty.

The other self can be reached only through the subconscious mind, and this irresistible entity with which everyone is
possessed is some mysterious power associated with, and exist-
ing on, the same plane as our unseen Guides.

This system of sleep treatment is especially adaptable to the
purpose of and the elimination of undesirable habits in children
while they sleep, and it can be put into operation without the
knowledge of the children.

"There is one quality which one must possess to win and that is: definiteness of purpose, the knowledge of what one wants, and a burning desire to possess it."

—*Think and Grow Rich*

The Eighth
Miracle of Life

NATURE'S DEFINITENESS OF PURPOSE
AND THE FIXATION OF NATURAL LAWS

THE FIXATION OF NATURAL LAWS is a miracle which forever safeguards all of Nature's plans and purposes and ensures that the overall plan of the universe will be carried out *without the possibility of interference from man.*

The Law of Cosmic Habitforce is the comptroller of all other natural laws and the power which gives fixation to all habits of every living thing in the lower orders of life than that of men, and fixes the habits of energy and matter as well as the distances and relationships between all the stars and planets.

Man alone has been provided with the privilege and the means by which he may fix his own habits, good or bad. The habits of all living things, on a lower plane of life, have been fixed by what we call "instinct," and the instinct pattern of each living thing on this lower plane represents the limitations and full extent of its activities.

Man's privilege to make and to break his own habits has been so definitely left in his own hands that he is not bound by any form of inherited limitations, such as are all lower forms of life. That great universal truth, "Whatever the mind of man can conceive and believe, the mind can achieve," is given sound foundation because of man's power to break all habits which have been fastened upon him by the Law of Cosmic Habitforce, and supplement them with other habits of his own choosing.

Once a man chooses a goal and creates plans for attaining it, Cosmic Habitforce will fix all his habits which are related to that goal so that they automatically lead him in the direction of the goal. However, man can break those habits at will, change his plans and his objectives, and set up an entirely new set of habits for the attainment of his objectives.

This power of choice in the selection and control of habits give man a rating *but one step below that of Infinite Intelligence*, and in fact, gives him the privilege of drawing upon the forces of Infinite Intelligence, at will, for the attainment of all his aims and purposes. For evidence to support this observation one has only to take inventory of man's achievements during the first half of the twentieth century, during which man caused to be revealed more of Nature's carefully hidden secrets than had been uncovered during the entire previous existence of mankind.

Step by step, by the exercise of his self-established habits of thought, man has ushered in the push-button age which permits him, figuratively speaking, to supply his every need by calmly sitting down and pushing buttons which set up vibrations in whatever direction he may desire.

Perhaps this evolutionary advancement of man, through which he has transferred to machines most of the labors he previously performed by hand, is only a part of Nature's plan of introducing man to his own mind power by the process of elimination. When there is no longer any need for the use of physical power, man will then have time to discover and use his brain power. And in that discovery he may learn that he can do all the things which the Nazarene challenged him to do: "*Even greater things than I have done.*"

The stars and planets, and the nebulous matter from which these were formed, are related to one another by Nature's habits of fixation, operating through the Law of Cosmic Habitforce. Day and night, the seasons of the year, the law of balance, and every living thing except man, are bound by inexorable habits which make their movements and actions accurately predictable over long periods of time and far in advance of the happenings.

Man alone has been given the privilege of fixing his own earthly destiny, with the right to make it pleasant and unpleasant, successful or unsuccessful, happy or unhappy, rich or poor, and his achievements are always unpredictable because his potential power is unlimited.

If man had but two more privileges than he now possesses he would be on an equal footing with the Creator: namely (1) the privilege of coming into the world at birth, of his own choice, and (2) the privilege of remaining among the living as long as he desired. Man has potential control of about everything else, but alas! He rarely discovers the powers available to him or makes any attempt to use those powers for his own uplift, or to make this a better world.

For the most part man settles down in a sort of tug-of-war struggle with forces which become unfriendly toward him because he does not understand them—forces such as the twelve miracles—and he gladly settles with life for a place to sleep, a little food to fill his belly, and enough clothes to hid his nakedness.

Once in a long while an individual steps out of the long procession of human beings, takes possession of his own mind, recognizes its powers, and makes use of them. Then the world has found an Edison, or a Ford, or a Luther Burbank, or an Alexander Graham Bell, or a Henry J. Kaiser—men who have removed all self-imposed limitations because they learned the truth that, "whatever the mind can conceive and believe, the mind can achieve."

Geniuses? Yes, because genius is simply a matter of self-discovery!

Know yourself—your other self which does not recognize limitations—and you may become "the master of your fate, the captain of your soul," and peace of mind will come to you as naturally as the eating of a meal when you are hungry.

Man's major weakness consists not of riches he does not possess, but in the *failure to make use of that which he has*! In every generation of people less than 1 percent of those who are living take over the torchlight of civilization and carry it over for the benefit of the next generation. Civilization is kept on the march by those who discover and make use of their own minds, the same is true in the average business enterprise, where a relatively small percentage of the individuals connected with the business are responsible for its successful operation. *The others are there in body but not in mind and spirit*, and often they take out of the business more than they contribute to it.

Nature does not vacillate, does not change her plans, and in this respect, she sets a beautiful example for people to follow. The successful ones do follow the example; *the failures do not.*

One of the impressive discoveries revealed to me during my contact with the successful men and women who helped me organize the Science of Success consisted of the fact that they moved with definiteness of purpose, and never wavered, slowed down, or quit when the going was hard. They succeeded because they knew what they desired, laid plans for attaining it, and followed those plans until they were rewarded with success.

I have often thought, when observing successful people who stick to their purpose through failure after failure, *that Infinite Intelligence throws itself on the side of the person who will not quit when obstacles have to be surmounted*; for somehow, these people always triumph eventually, no matter how many handicaps they have to master.

When I first heard that Thomas A. Edison had surmounted more than ten thousand failures before he found the secret of the incandescent electric lamp, I wondered how any human being could or would pay such a high price for victory. Later, after I became intimately acquainted with the Edison mind, and the method with which he applied it to the solution of his problems, *I discovered that it was the disciplinary effects of those ten thousand failures which made Edison the greatest inventor of all times.*

Edison must have recognized, as he met with one failure after another, that persistence would eventually bring him the secret he was seeking. I am led to this conclusion because of my own experiences in times of failure, when I was searching for the causes of success and failure, for each failure with which I met had only the effect of making me more determined to keep on until I met with success. That small still voice which speaks to one from within kept telling me not to quit when I was overtaken by defeat.

If we could only experience, for a single time, the hurts of both the physical and mental pains felt by those who go through the period of struggle before they meet with victory in the upper brackets of human achievements. We would be utterly ashamed to admit the fear of so trivial an experience as that of dental or surgical operations.

*"Money is shy and elusive. It must be wooed
and won by methods not unlike those used by a
determined lover, in pursuit of the girl of his choice."*

—*Think and Grow Rich*

The Ninth
Miracle of Life

HOW TO TRANSMUTE
THE CREATIVE FORCE OF SEX

THE CREATIVE POWER OF SEX EMOTION is a subject the ignorance of which has set civilization backward a thousand years. The true story of sex is one of romance unequaled in any of Nature's other devices for the perpetuation of the world in which we live and the universe of which we are an infinite part.

Because the emotion of sex has been burlesqued and profaned by the vulgar minded until the very word "sex" is seldom mentioned in mixed company, I shall here present some of its rare virtues not generally mentioned in sex literature or by teachers of this subject. The reason for this omission is fear that those who speak of sex will be suspicioned of possessing some queer quirk of the mind which makes them unacceptable in society.

For my own part I shall hew to the line of truth as I see it and let the "quips" fall wherever the uninformed minds may drop them. The brief interpretation of Sex Emotion I have here presented is the result of more than forty years of study of the subject of sex, much of which was carried on in collaboration with doctors and psychiatrists of recognized character and professional ability, some of it through my own experience in the work of counseling individuals in the application of the Science of Success.

It is a little-known fact that transmuted sex emotion may be, and it often is, a powerful factor in the achievement of success in all businesses, professions, and callings.

The following facts concerning sex emotion are worthy of careful analysis:

1. During the sexual engagement the door to the subconscious mind is wide open and any desires, aims, or purposes expressed at that time are instantly picked up by the subconscious and often acted upon with astounding speed. Therefore, a Master Mind alliance between a man and his wife can best be expressed for the attainment of any desired purpose, by clearly describing the purpose during sexual contact.

2. To get the best results from plans and purposes expressed to the subconscious mind during sexual contact, the engagement should be prolonged from one to three hours before a climax is reached. During this time both partners to the relationship should orally describe any plan or purpose desired to be acted upon by the subconscious mind. Best results will come from

expressing these desires or plans at and for five to ten minutes after the climax has been reached.

3. The emotion of sex has therapeutic values unequaled by anything known to man. The treatment consists of directing the minds of both partners during the entire sexual engagement to the correction of either physical or mental ailments. By this method every one of the body cells is recharged with bodily resistance, and all the organs of the body are alerted and put into speeded-up action in performing their normal duties. This system may be used for the correction of mental or physical ailments, but more important than this it may be used to keep the body charged with the health-giving forces of Nature.

4. The sex engagement should be carried on with oral expressions of love and affection stepped up to a high crescendo of emotion. This has the effect of arousing and alerting all the cells and all the organs of the body.

5. For the reasons here stated the sexual engagement offers the most favorable circumstances under which the mind may be conditioned for any desired purposes: for the attainment of success in connection with one's calling, the restoration of mental and physical health, the mastery of fear and melancholy, and the elimination of any undesirable habits such as the habit of smoking and alcoholism. It is also the most favorable circumstance under which to build desirable habits, such as the most favorable circumstances under which to build desirable habits, such as a success

consciousness, a health consciousness, or the development of any desired traits of character.

6. To get the best results from Sex Transmutation by
    the method here described, the sex partners should
    practice self-discipline until they can reach a climax
    at approximately the same moment; also, until they
    can prolong the climax for any time they choose.
    Premature climax on the part of either partner to the
    engagement will destroy much of the magnetic power
    which would otherwise be available for giving instruc-
    tions to the subconscious mind. If such a premature
    climax should be experienced by either of the partners,
    the sex engagement should be begun anew and fol-
    lowed through to a simultaneous climax by both.

7. Any suggested plans or purposes planted in the sub-
    conscious mind during sexual engagements carried on
    under the method herein described, *for not less than
    once a day for ten consecutive days*, will definitely be
    acted upon by the subconscious in the form of ways
    and means being transmitted to one or both of the sex
    partners, for the attainment of those plans or purposes.

8. Both parties to the sexual engagement should express
    themselves both physically and orally, in a well-bal-
    anced physical movement, attuned to their oral expres-
    sions. Each oral expression should be emphasized by
    a physical movement. If the physical movements are
    left entirely or largely, to one or the other of the sex
    partners, the one who refrains from physical action
    will be cheated of his or her proper share of the sex
    magnetism.

A well balanced, properly conducted sexual engagement steps up, intensifies, and balances, equally, the sex magnetism of the two partners. *If this balance is not maintained, eventually one or the other of the partners will suffer some form of mental or physical disturbance!* Doctors are quite familiar with this widespread cause of one or the other of the sex partners being sapped of a major portion of his or her sex magnetism, and consequently being left unprotected from physical and mental disturbances, because of insufficiency of bodily resistance.

9. Preparations for sexual contact should be arranged with great care as to time, place of the engagement, personal attire, and freedom of the minds of both partners from all disturbing influences of whatsoever nature. Remember, *the state of mind of the contacting partners during sexual intercourse goes directly to the subconscious mind of the contacting partners and is there translated into its material equivalent through subsequent guidance* by the subconscious minds of the partners.

10. The period of sexual intercourse provides the most favorable time and circumstances under which to express one's desire in the form of prayers, provided the method herein described is followed.

11. So far, we have been describing Sex Transmutation through physical sexual intercourse, which is by far the most effective way to transmute sex magnetism. However, there is another method by which Sex Emotion may be transmuted into any desired objective. It consists of the individual working himself or herself

into an intense desire for sexual intercourse and then switching that desire to any form of action necessary to carry out one's business, professional or occupational purposes. This method is often used where sexual compatibility is lacking in one of the sex partners.

There is still another method of overcoming the lack of sexual compatibility. It consists of vicarious substitution by which the one who lacks the compatibility is supplanted in the imagination of the other sex partner by some other person chosen by and suitable to the other sex partner. This substitution can easily be adopted by the simple process of closing one's eyes and seeing, in his imagination, any sex partner whom he may have chosen. This method is often resorted to in preference to illegitimate sex relations by men and women whose sex partners are not compatible.

Men and women who are not compatible with their sex partners, or have lost this compatibility through illness or otherwise, often follow the habit of simulating sex passion which they do not actually feel. This is a poor substitute, but serves better than no substitute at all. (When none of these methods are satisfactory, doctors sometimes recommend the temporary changing of sex partners where patients from physical or mental ailments are suffering because of the lack of a balanced sexual relationship. This fact is never mentioned because the method does not harmonize with accepted social and moral standards, but doctors sometimes wisely go beyond the common practices in social and moral relationships in order to restore health, and not infrequently this extreme method is adopted with the full knowledge and consent of both the sex partners.)

I have, on a few occasions, recommended the temporary change of sex partners as a means of developing a success consciousness in my students, but always this has been done with the full consent of both partners, and generally where the student has become so thoroughly mastered by a poverty or an inferiority complex that extreme methods had to be applied to break that consciousness.

Regarding the false notion that sex expression is a sin: The expression of sex, under natural conditions, as herein described, is the highest form of human intercourses. It is a sin only when engaged in for pleasurable purposes, *but never a sin when indulged in for creative purposes*. It is not a sin when it is motivated by the emotion of Love. It is never a sin when motivated by the desire for worthy achievements in one's business, profession, or calling. It is never a sin when motivated by the purpose of maintaining or regaining physical or mental health.

The emotion of sex is older than marriage, it is older than religion, it is the clever device by which the Creator maintains the perpetuation of all living things, from the lowest to the highest, *and it is a sin only when perverted from the noble purposes of the Creator*.

Ignorance on the subject of sexual relations heads the list of causes of incompatibility and infelicity in the marriage relationship. Ignorance is particularly widespread in connection with the subject of timing of the climax of the sexual engagement.

Ignorance on the subject of sexual relations and marriage relations in general is so widespread that there is a growing need for schools where those who contemplate marriage can get the training they need to make the marriage successful. The schools should be conducted by both male and female teachers with extensive experience and training in all subjects taught. And many of those who are already married might well discover a new and a better way of living together if they took a course in a marriage school.

Schools of marriage should give students a thorough analysis of the following subjects:

1. A complete description of the purposes of the sexual relation, as herein stated, with a detailed statement of the technique which will enable the partners to rise to the highest degree of ecstasy during the engagement and reach a climax at approximately the same moment. Timing is very important and it calls for a complete understanding of both partners.

    During my twenty years of research in the organization of the Science of Success I had the privilege of working closely with more than five hundred of the top-ranking successful men and women of America. It became quite obvious that the main difference between these successful people and the average run of people who never attain noteworthy success consisted in the fact that they were *highly sexed and they had learned the art of Sex Transmutation*. (Sex Transmutation has reference to the individual's habit of directing the profound creative forces of sex emotion to the attainment of his occupation, aims, and plans, *and receiving from his success achievements the same gratification he would have received from a sexual climax had his energies been directed to that end*. This statement does not mean that the individual must practice sexual abstinence except at such times as he may desire to temporarily direct this creative force to other ends than intercourse through physical contact.)

Mind conditioning, for any purpose whatsoever, is most quickly and effectively attained during sexual intercourse. There is no other time or circumstance which equals it, a statement which can be easily verified by experiment. Let it be emphasized, however, that *both parties to the transaction must be in perfect harmony*, both must practice and self-discipline at the beginning.

2. Instructions on the importance of the time, the place, and the physical environment in preparation for sexual engagement.

3. A complete program on home economy, including the budgeting of income and expenses, with an allowance for the wife's personal spending which does not need to be accounted for. No wife will long respect a husband who is so unthoughtful of her financial needs that she is forced to steal a little change from his pockets while he sleeps or has to hold out a few nickels and dimes from the egg and butter money in order that she may have a few unmentionables or hair ribbons.

4. A complete training in social relations so that no unnecessary social obligations are incurred. Particular emphasis should be focused on the necessity for care in the selection of social acquaintances.

5. Training in the proper method of blending the minds of the husband and wife in a Master Mind alliance, as described in the Science of Success. This portion of the marriage school training might well eliminate one of

the major causes for dissension in marriages, namely, the lack of adequate financial means.

6. An elementary course in biology which, if properly presented, would remove that old false notion that all forms of sexual relation are sinful. Every person, whether married or single, should have at least an elementary working knowledge of the great creative forces of sex. As a matter of fact, this knowledge should be imparted to children at a very early age. And thus saving them from getting their sex information from unreliable and unsavory sources, which often makes of sex a "hush hush" subject and a thing of indecency instead of a profound, creative device with which all living things are perpetuated.

7. Extensive training in the psychology of child management, including instructions on how to secure discipline with the full, enthusiastic cooperation of the child instead of commanding it by fears and threats.

8. Training on how young married couples should relate themselves to their relatives and in-laws.

9. Instructions on how husband and wife should relate themselves to each other on the subject of religion where their respective religions are of a different denomination.

Schools of marriage might well become a function of the churches since this would remove from them the suspicion that they may in some instances be inadequately chaperoned or there might be an adjunct to the public school system.

We are living in an age when man has mastered the air above us and the sea beneath us; he has revealed the principle of radio, radar, the X-ray, the telephone, and wireless means of communication, and he has isolated and conquered many of the sources of physical and mental ailments, but with all of his revelations of the secrets of Nature, man has not yet fully explored or availed himself of the great creative forces of sex nor of the boundless potentialities of the human mind.

And the layman or the scientist who discovers the stupendous possibilities of individual achievement, by means of coordination of the principle of sex and the control of the mind, will give the world a new birth in the form of a new and better system of human relations, including a simple technique by which an individual may quickly condition his mind for the attainment of any desired purpose.

We have learned a lot about machines, guns, and explosives with which whole cities may be wiped out instantly, but the greatest of all forces, "mental dynamite," is yet to be explored and adapted to man's struggle for existence.

Life may be a magnificent interlude of joyous growth and unfoldment, which the Creator probably intended it to be, or a period of misery and maladjustment in human relations, with a flock of worries as the payoff for the struggles we make in order to live. The deciding factor as to which of this life shall be, is under the control of the individual, and it represents the most profound of all the gifts of the Creator. It consists of controlling his own mind, which is the irrevocable privilege every individual has.

"Time is the friend of the person who trains his mind to follow positive thought-habits and the enemy of the person who drifts into negative thought-habits."

—Outwitting the Devil

The Tenth Miracle of Life

TIME, NATURE'S UNIVERSAL CURE FOR ALL HUMAN ILLS

TIME is the great Universal Doctor of human ills whose chief agent is the ether, the energy which connects everything with every other thing in the universe.

TIME is the great healer of wounds, both physical and mental, and it is the transformer of all *causes* into their *appropriate effects.*

TIME trades irrational youth for maturity of age and wisdom!

TIME transmutes the wounds of the heart and the frustrations of our daily lives into courage, endurance, and understanding. Without this kindly and beneficent service most individuals would be lost in the early days of their youth.

TIME ripens the grain in the fields and the fruit of the trees and makes them ready for human enjoyment and sustenance.

TIME gives hot heads a chance to cool off and become rational.

TIME helps us discover the great laws of Nature, by the trial and error method, and to profit by our mistakes of judgment.

TIME is our most precious possession because we can be sure of no more than a single second of it on any given date or place.

TIME is the agent of mercy through which we may repeat of our sins and errors and gain useful knowledge therefrom.

TIME favors those who interpret Nature's laws correctly and who adapt them as guideposts to the correct habits of living, but *time* swings heavily with penalties for those who ignore or neglect these laws.

TIME is the master manipulator of the universal law of Cosmic Habitforce, the fixer of all habits, both of living creatures and inanimate things.

TIME is also the master manipulator of the lesser law of compensation, through the operation of which everyone reaps that which he sows. (The positive operation of this law is called the law of increasing returns; the negative operation is called the law of diminishing returns.)

TIME does not always operate the law of compensation swiftly, but it does operate definitely, according to fixed habits and patterns which the philosopher understands, and by which he can foretell the nature of coming events by examining the *cause* from which they are to spring.

TIME is also the master manipulator of the great Law of Change which keeps all things and all people in a constant state of flux, and never allows them to remain the same for two minutes of succession. This truth is laden with benefits of stupendous proportions because it provides the means by which we may correct our mistakes, eliminate our false fears and weak habits, and exchange ignorance for wisdom and peace of mind as we grow older.

Go back into your past experiences and take count of the occasions when your troubled heart found no surcease from its aches save only by the merciful hand of Doctor Time.

If you have failed in business or in some occupational undertaking which you chose as your life work, you may have observed that TIME came to your rescue with other and perhaps greater opportunities, and you rejoiced that you had been detoured from your course to a smoother and broader highway of opportunity.

On the next occasion when you find yourself wasting a single second of this precious agent of OPPORTUNITY, TIME, copy the following resolution, commit it to memory, and start immediately to carry it out.

My Commitment to Doctor Time!

1. Time is my greatest asset, and I shall relate myself to it on a budget system which provides that every second not devoted to sleep shall be used for self-improvement.
2. In the future, I shall regard the loss, through neglect, of any portion of my Time as a sin, for which I must atone by the better use in the future of an equivalent amount of it.
3. Recognizing that I shall reap that which I sow, I shall sow only the seeds of service which may benefit others as well as myself, and thereby throw myself in the way of the great Law of Compensation.

4. I shall so use my Time in the future that each day brings me some measure of peace of mind, in the absence of which I shall recognize that the seed I have been sowing needs reexamination.

5. Knowing that my habits of thought become the patterns which attract all the circumstances affecting my life through the lapse of Time. I will keep my mind so busy in connection with the circumstances I *desire* that no Time will be left to devote to fears and frustrations, and the things *I do not desire.*

6. Recognizing that at best my allotted Time on the earth plane is indefinite and limited, I shall endeavor in all ways possible to use my portion of it so that those nearest me will benefit by my influence and be inspired by my example to make the best possible use of their own Time.

7. Finally, when my allotment of Time shall have expired, I hope I may leave behind me a monument to my name, not a monument in stone, but in the hearts of my fellowmen—a monument whose marking will testify that the world was made a little better because of my having passed this way.

8. I will repeat this Commitment daily during the remainder of my allotment of Time, and back it with BELIEF that it will improve my character and inspire those whom I may influence, to likewise improve their lives.

The hands of the Clock of Time are moving swiftly onward! We cry out, "Backward, turn backward O Time in your flight," but Time does not heed our cries.

It is later than you think! Arouse yourself, fellow wayfarer; awake and take possession of your own mind while you still have enough Time to become, during the yet unexpired future, that which you would have liked to have been in the past. Make the most of your present allotment of Time with the hope that you will not have to reincarnate in order to do the job all over again because of neglect. You have been warned!

Now the responsibility is YOURS. There is a simple test by which you may judge whether or not you have been using your Time to your best advantage. If you have attained peace of mind and material opulence sufficient for your needs, your Time has been properly used. If you have not attained these blessings, your Time has not been properly used, and you should begin now to search for the circumstances in connection with which you have fallen short.

The truly great people have no such reality as "idle time," because they keep their minds geared eternally to patterns of constructive thought. By this profound use of their Time they develop an alert sixth sense through which they look. Listen and see from within.

If negative thoughts stray into the minds of the truly great, these thoughts are immediately transmuted into positive thoughts and exercised by positive physical action appropriate to their nature.

Tick, tick, tick—the pendulum of the Clock of Time is swinging rapidly!

The entire face of civilization is undergoing an uplifting operation.

Mr. Right and Mr. Wrong are engaged in mortal combat for supremacy. The Time has come for everyone to stand up and be counted. The use each of us makes of his individual allotment of time will tell whose side that he is on, Mr. Right's or Mr. Wrong's.

Something has speeded up the Clock of Time so rapidly that the last half of the twentieth century will reveal to mankind more individual opportunities for self-improvement than have been revealed during the entire past of man's existence.

Your share of these vast *OPPORTUNITIES* may be embraced and used only by the way you relate yourself to TIME!

*"Men and women who come to the closing chapter
of life disappointed because they did not attain
the goal which they had set their hearts upon
achieving, they teach you what not to do."*

—Outwitting the Devil

The Eleventh
Miracle of Life

WISDOM ROBS DEATH OF ITS STING

THE MYSTERY OF DEATH: It may be difficult for most people to interpret Death as being anything but an unavoidable tragedy, but this limited view of the subject can be broadened by taking account of the overall plan of the universe, which is in a constant state of flux, constantly undergoing eternal change.

Man comes to the earth plane without his knowledge or consent, remains in the Great School of Life a little while, then passes into another plane of intelligence without his consent. It is not a part of the Creator's plan for man to live on the earth plane forever, and it would be a tragedy if it were a part of that plan. Could anyone think of anything more frightful than to be compelled to remain forever on this earth plane of struggle, where life itself depends upon eternal vigilance on the part of the individual?

The life span is something like the modern school system. We enter the kindergarten period, graduate from there into the grades, then into high school, and from there we enter the last stage by entering college. The major purpose behind man's brief interlude on earth seems to be that of education.

If there had been no device of Death, think of the evil men the world has known, men who would still be living and making life miserable for everyone, the would-be conquerors and self-appointed dictators who have sought, from the dawn of civilization, to subjugate all mankind.

Death is but an extended form of sleep, during which the individual sheds his tired, worn-out physical body for one that is inexhaustible and eternal. Therefore, it is a circumstance over which the individual has no final control, and it should be accepted as such and dismissed from the mind.

Understand the Law of Change, which is a part of the universal system, and Death becomes understandable and may be readily accepted as a necessity. There could not coexist in the universe an eternal Law of Change and eternal life on the earth plane.

The individual may fear death, dread to meet with it, and look upon it as a tragedy, but fortunately the individual is only a pawn in relation to the overall plan of the universe, and as such his desire and the means of their fulfillment are confined entirely to that brief interlude known as Life, over which the individual has been given a free hand, to spend his brief visit in whatever manner he pleases.

The attitude of the philosopher toward Death seems to be the sensible one. He accepts it as a circumstance over which he has but a slight, limited control; therefore, he adjusts himself to it in a neutral spirit of belief that when it comes, he will be ready for it, and he then dismisses the subject and devotes his energies to making his life yield all the benefits he can *in connection with those circumstances over which he has control.*

The philosopher looks upon those who fear Death as offering insult to their Creator. And the philosopher accepts every circumstance which touches his life as grist for the mill of life, and promptly adjusts himself to all such circumstances in a manner best suited to enable him to benefit by them.

Some of the great miracles constitute the major impediments standing in the way of peace of mind of the majority of people. The purpose of this analysis of the Miracles is to help the individual relate himself to them in a mental attitude which will change them from things to be dreaded to circumstances which can be made beneficial to his interests.

Through this analysis of the Twelve Great Miracles, the "Worry Bird" (which most people feed unnecessarily) has been robbed of the food necessary to keep it alive and this way has been cleared of peace of mind, based on the acceptance of all the circumstances of life, just as they are.

It is my hope that each of you who reads this volume will be conditioned, upon finishing this chapter, to properly interpret and apply the principles set forth in these chapters, which have been designed to help you relate yourself to the Miracles in a manner that will give you the greatest benefits.

When this hope shall have been realized, then you will have found peace of mind which will endure throughout the remainder of life.

The statements I have made in this analysis are not important. *But the thinking on your part which the statements may have inspired is important!* For it may well be that the thinking thus inspired may give you a change of attitude toward Life, which will make Life sweeter as the years grow fewer.

"Success comes to those who become success conscious."

—*Think and Grow Rich*

The Twelfth Miracle of Life

THE AMERICAN WAY OF LIFE
MAKES MEN FREE
(ONE OF THE GREAT MIRACLES OF ALL TIMES)

FREEDOM OF THE AMERICAN WAY OF LIFE is one of the Great Miracles of all times. Here in the United States of America the stage has been set and the way has been prepared, as nowhere else on this earth at any period of time, for man to take full and complete possession of his own mind and direct it to whatever ends he may desire.

Our American Way of Life was born by the shedding of tears of blood and matured through hardship and struggle which touched the lives of every living citizen of the nation, which indicates that our way of Life harmonizes in every particular with the Creator's plan to allow all men to become free by the exercise of their own minds.

Evidence that ours is a land of OPPORTUNITY, where any person may choose his own objective in life and achieve it, through the operation of his own mind, is available in overwhelming abundance. Where else on earth except in America could an uneducated Italian immigrant such as A. P. Giannini start his career by pushing a banana cart and pyramid his efforts into the ownership of the world's largest banking system?

Where else but in America could a young, uneducated mechanic give birth to an industry like that of the automobile industry, and without capital to begin with, pyramid his humble beginning into a worldwide empire with a fabulous fortune, and provide employment for hundreds of thousands of people as Henry Ford did?

And where except in the United States does the humblest laborer enjoy more of the modern convenience of living than did kings and potentates a few generations ago?

Where else on earth except in the United States is every citizen provided with adequate motives of self-aggrandizing sufficient to inspire him to act on his own personal initiative, choose his own career, think his own thoughts, and express them in any manner he chooses?

Where else is every male child born as a potential holder of the highest office the people have to offer, and where else has such a high office been successfully administered by a humble rail-splitter?

Where except in the United States of America can any individual of any race or creed walk with dignity upon the earth and say, truly, "I am free?"

Where except in America could an uneducated lad choose as his career the business of inventing, surround himself with a

Master Mind of scientifically skilled men, and make himself the greatest inventor of all times, as did Thomas A. Edison?

I have posed these questions for you, who enjoy the largess of the great American Way of Life, with the hope that you who read this volume will answer them, each in his own way, according to the benefits this country may have provided him, and in searching your own hearts and minds for the answers, learn to better evaluate the vast opportunities open to *you* in any calling you may choose.

Before we leave this analysis of the Great American Way of Life, let us be reminded that this heritage will remain ours only so long as we recognize it, use it properly, and protect it. Like all other blessings conferred upon man by Mother Nature, our rights to the privileges we enjoy in America will remain only as long as we earn the right to them. Nature looks with great disfavor on the idea of *something for nothing.*

Appendix

FATHER DIVINE

Father Divine, born George Baker around 1876, was a prominent religious leader in the early to mid-twentieth century who founded the International Peace Mission Movement. He is best known for his role as a charismatic preacher who claimed to be God incarnate, offering a message of equality, economic independence, and communal living to his followers. His influence extended beyond his religious teachings, as he played a significant role in the social and economic life of African Americans during the Great Depression and beyond.

Father Divine's early life is somewhat shrouded in mystery, with few reliable records documenting his origins. He was born in Rockville, Maryland, and worked as a gardener and a butler in his early years. His religious journey began in the early 1900s, when he became involved with a number of religious groups, including the Holiness movement and various Pentecostal churches. By the 1910s, he had begun to attract followers through his charismatic preaching and claims of divinity, adopting the name "Father Divine."

In 1919, Father Divine settled in Sayville, Long Island, where he established a communal living arrangement for his followers, known as the Peace Mission. This community emphasized racial integration, a radical concept at the time, and practiced communal sharing of resources. Father Divine preached a gospel of economic independence, urging his followers to rely on their own labor and to shun charity. His message was particularly appealing to African Americans, who faced severe economic hardships and racial discrimination during this period.

The 1930s marked a period of significant growth for Father Divine's movement. The Great Depression had devastated the American economy, leaving millions unemployed and destitute. Father Divine's Peace Mission offered an alternative to the prevailing social and economic order, providing food, shelter, and employment to those in need. He established a network of communal homes, businesses, and farms that were collectively owned and operated by his followers. These enterprises were remarkably successful, allowing the Peace Mission to become largely self-sufficient and to provide for its members' needs.

Father Divine's teachings were grounded in a belief in the inherent divinity of all people, which he expressed through his own claim to be God. He preached that God was present on earth in the form of his own body and that by following him, his followers could achieve eternal life. This claim was central to his movement and set him apart from other religious leaders of the time. His teachings also emphasized the importance of living a moral and upright life, free from sin, and he enforced strict codes of conduct within his communities.

Father Divine relocated his headquarters to Harlem, New York, where his movement continued to grow. In Harlem, Father Divine expanded his network of communal homes and businesses, and his influence grew even further. He opened "heavens," which were dining halls that served inexpensive meals to both followers and the needy. These heavens became a crucial resource for many during the Depression, providing food and a sense of community to thousands. Father Divine's emphasis on racial integration and economic self-sufficiency resonated with African Americans in Harlem, who were often excluded from mainstream economic opportunities.

Father Divine's impact extended beyond his religious teachings. He was a vocal advocate for civil rights and social justice, and his movement played a role in the broader struggle for African American equality. He encouraged his followers to boycott businesses that practiced racial discrimination and to support African American–owned enterprises. His teachings on economic independence also influenced later movements, such as the Black Power movement of the 1960s, which emphasized self-reliance and economic empowerment.

Father Divine passed away in 1965, but his movement continued under the leadership of his second wife, known as Mother Divine. Although the Peace Mission Movement has declined significantly since its peak in the 1930s and 1940s, it still exists today, with a small number of followers dedicated to preserving Father Divine's legacy.

Father Divine was a complex and influential figure whose impact on American religious and social life was profound.

His teachings on racial equality, economic independence, and communal living offered a powerful alternative to the dominant social and economic structures of his time. While his claims of divinity were controversial, they were central to his appeal and to the sense of community he fostered among his followers. Father Divine's legacy continues to be felt in the ongoing struggle for social and economic justice in the United States.

Napoleon Hill Timeline

1883—Napoleon Hill is born on October 26, 1883, in Wise County in Southwest Virginia, a rural, poverty-stricken area of the United States.

1893—Napoleon's mother, Sara Blair, dies at age twenty-four.

1894—Napoleon's father marries Martha Ramey. She was a schoolteacher and greatly influenced Napoleon's love for writing. She bought him a typewriter when he was thirteen.

1898—Napoleon begins writing for small rural newspapers as a "mountain reporter."

1900–1902—Napoleon graduates from high school, leaves Wise County to attend business school in Tazewell, Virginia, graduates, and is employed by prominent Virginia lawyer Rufus Ayres, eventually managing a coal mine for Ayres.

1903–1908—Napoleon attends law school, but does not finish, and becomes a sales manager at a lumberyard until economic conditions worsen and he returns to seeking work as a journalist.

1908—Napoleon interviews Andrew Carnegie, one of the world's richest men, as part a series on famous men for *Bob Taylor's Magazine*. Carnegie urges Napoleon to devote twenty years of his life to develop a philosophy of success.

1908–1928—Napoleon interviews over 500 successful men in every industry, including Thomas Edison, Henry Ford, Charles Schwab, Alexander Graham Bell, Theodore Roosevelt, John Wanamaker, Elmer Gates, Woodrow Wilson, William Jennings Bryan, John D. Rockefeller, George Eastman, Edward W. Bok, William H. Taft, Jennings Randolph, Luther Burbank, Julius Rosenwal, Clarence Darrow, and William Wrigley, Jr.

1910—Napoleon marries Florence Horner.

1911–1918—Napoleon's son James is born in 1911, followed by Napoleon Blair in 1912, and finally, David in 1918.

1919–1920—Napoleon founds, edits and publishes *Hill's Golden Rule* magazine.

1928—Napoleon's first published book, *The Law of Success*, is released in 1928. It is an eight-volume set developed from Napoleon's interviews of successful men; it is his first study course to outline his "Philosophy of Achievement."

1930—*The Magic Ladder of Success*, Napoleon's second book, is published.

1931—Napoleon founds, edits, publishes, and closes after two issues *Inspiration* magazine.

1937—*Think and Grow Rich*, Napoleon's famous and influential self-help book, is released and becomes the best-selling personal success guide of all-time.

1938—Napoleon writes *Outwitting the Devil*, but considered too controversial for its time, the manuscript is not published until 2011.

1941—*Mental Dynamite* volume one study course is released, and though a sold-out success, further planned volumes are not published due to wartime paper rationing.

1943—Napoleon marries his third wife, Annie Lou Norman.

1945—*The Master-Key to Riches* is published.

1952–1962—Napoleon meets W. Clement Stone, founder of Combined Insurance Company of America. Mr. Stone becomes Napoleon's general manager and they travel around the country promoting the success philosophy.

1962—The Napoleon Hill Foundation is formed to continue Napoleon's work of making the world a better place in which to live.

1970— On November 8, 1970, Napoleon Hill dies at his home in South Carolina at age eighty-seven.

1971—*You Can Work Your Own Miracles* is posthumously published by the Napoleon Hill Foundation.

2025—*The 12 Miracles of Life*, written between 1949 and 1965, is rediscovered and posthumously published by Humanix Books.

Editor NAPOLEON HILL'S MAGAZINE

About the Author

Napoleon Hill was born in a log cabin on the Pound River in Wise County, Virginia, on October 26, 1883. Napoleon was the firstborn child of Sara and James Hill.

Napoleon Hill was born at a time when one- and two-room log cabins were typical dwellings and life in general was primitive when compared to today's standards. Life expectancies were short, infant mortality was high, and many rural Virginians suffered from chronic health problems.

At the time of Hill's birth, elementary schools were open only about four months out of the year and attendance was not required.

James Monroe Hill, Napoleon's father, was the son of James Madison Hill, an English-born printer who immigrated to America in the 1840s with two brothers and settled in the Black Mountain area on the Kentucky–Virginia border.

By the age of seventeen James had married Sara Sylvania Blair and built a cabin in a remote area. James made a press and began publication of *Zephyr*, Wise County's first newspaper. The *Zephyr* contained personals, local news, weather, and a brief editorial. The newspaper was delivered by horseback to about one hundred subscribers in the area.

James and Sara Hill named their first son Oliver Napoleon. Oliver was later dropped from Napoleon's name.

Napoleon's earliest years marked him for anything but success. He was a wild, perhaps hyperactive, child known to neighbors and family members mainly for the mischief he caused. By Hill's own account, his parents started him in school at age four "mainly to get me off their hands while they worked in the fields."

Little is known of Sara Hill, prior to her death, except that she had borne Napoleon and his brother Vivian. Napoleon was the young age of nine when he lost his mother. At nine, Napoleon considered himself the toughest boy in the county and was a serious disciplinary problem for this father.

Napoleon's penchant for pranks and mischief took on a more foreboding direction following the death of his mother. In the mountain region where it was common for young boys to hunt with rifles, Napoleon began carrying a six-shooter he inherited from an uncle. Napoleon imagined himself to be Jesse James, not the best hero to select to worship at any age especially as an unsettled nine-year-old.

One year after the death of Sara Hill, James married Martha Ramey Banner, the widow of a school principal and daughter of a Coeburn, Virginia, physician. Martha Hill was a well-educated and dynamic woman, and she had announced that she intended to change the mental, spiritual, and financial status of the entire family.

When Napoleon was eleven years old, his stepmother suggested he devote his time to reading and writing and concluded, "you mighty live to see the time when your influence will be felt throughout the state." By the age of twelve Napoleon was convinced by his stepmother to give up his gun for a typewriter.

Napoleon Hill popularized the phrase, "what the mind can conceive, it can achieve." Martha Hill was greatly responsible for the growth of young Napoleon's mind, and it can be stated that

Napoleon Hill, like Abraham Lincoln, owed whatever greatness would come to each was due to their stepmothers' loving care and influence.

At the age of thirteen Napoleon took his first paying job after he got out of school as a laborer in the coal mines. Coal mining was a dirty, hard job which Napoleon, at one dollar a day wages, quickly learned that coal mining was not a future that he desired.

By the age of fifteen Napoleon became a news reporter in the mountains of Wise County and saw this as an excellent choice to replace one of working in the coal mines or farming.

Napoleon attended Gladville High School, which was a two-year high school at the time, and finished at the age of seventeen. He then left Wise County to attend business school in Tazewell, Virginia.

Upon graduation from business school, Napoleon went to work for Rufus Ayers, a prominent attorney who had been the attorney general of Virginia and was one of the wealthiest men in Wise County in 1901. Ayers was involved in coal mining, the lumber business, and banking. He built a mansion in Big Stone Gap that today houses the Southwest Museum. Working for Attorney General Ayers, Napoleon was a fast success and fit in the business world at a quick pace. In less than six months Napoleon was promoted to chief clerk of a coal mine in Richlands, Virginia. While working for Rufus Ayers, Napoleon had been encouraged by Mr. Ayers to study law, which had great appeal for Napoleon.

Napoleon, along with his brother Vivian, attended Georgetown Law School in Washington, D.C., and while attending school went to work for Robert L. Taylor, a former governor who published *Bob Taylor's Magazine*. While working for Bob Taylor, Napoleon agreed to begin working on interviewing successful businesspeople. At the age of twenty-five he found himself at the mansion of Andrew Carnegie, and it was that interview that defined the balance of Napoleon's life.

Andrew Carnegie challenged young Napoleon to develop a philosophy of success by interviewing successful people and learn from them. He inspired Napoleon to write it down for others to follow.

During Napoleon's study of success, which lasted over twenty years, he interviewed most of the highly successful individuals in the United States—both in business and government. He later became an advisor to Presidents Franklin Roosevelt and Woodrow Wilson.

In 1937 Napoleon wrote *Think and Grow Rich*, which has sold in excess of twenty-five million copies. Napoleon had other successful books, all of which have made millionaires of more people than one can imagine with a philosophy that is still followed today by many of the world's most successful people—and whose influence is felt all over the world.

Before Napoleon's death in November of 1970, the Napoleon Hill Foundation was established in 1962 as a nonprofit charitable educational institution dedicated to making the world a better place to live!

To learn more, go to NapHill.org.

Don M. Green is executive director of the Napoleon Hill Foundation and president of the foundation board at the University of Virginia—Wise. He became CEO of Black Diamond Savings Bank at forty-one and studied under personal development master W. Clement Stone. He travels extensively, lecturing worldwide for the foundation. Most recently, Mr. Green was featured in a United Nations forum on the importance of entrepreneurship within the national economy.

Green's first youthful business venture was charging admission to see his pet bear—yes, the living, growling kind! Since 2000, Green has traveled worldwide and used his finance skills to grow the Napoleon Hill Foundation's funds in order to continue the foundation's educational outreach to prisons. Green has both modeled leadership skills as a CEO and taught them through the PMA Science of Success course at the University of Virginia's College at Wise. Don specializes in discussing his personal experiences in leadership and providing audiences with proven methods of applying Dr. Hill's success philosophy to business.

Green brings nearly forty-five years of banking, finance, and entrepreneurship experience to his role as executive director of the Napoleon Hill Foundation, and is the author of *Napoleon Hill's Secret, Everything I Know About Success I Learned from Napoleon Hill, Napoleon Hill My Mentor, Napoleon Hill's Your Millionaire Mindset,* and *The Gift of Giving.*

Visit The Napoleon Hill Foundation to learn even more about Napoleon Hill, his legacy and philosophy of success at NapHill.org.

NAPOLEON HILL'S WORDS OF WISDOM TO INSPIRE SUCCESS IN WORK AND LIFE

You can do it if you think you can.

When riches begin to come, they come so quickly and in such great abundance that one wonders where they have been hiding all those lean years.

When defeat comes, accept it as a signal that your plans are not sound, rebuild those plans, and set sail once more toward your coveted goal.

Poverty needs no plan. It needs no one to aid it, because it is bold and ruthless.

Every adversity, every unpleasant experience, every failure, carries with it the seed of an equivalent or greater benefit.

To be a star, you must shine your own light, follow your own path, and don't worry about darkness, for that is when the stars shine brightest.

Sometimes it appears there is a hidden guide whose duty is to test people through all sorts of discouraging experiences. Those who pick themselves up after defeat and keep on trying arrive. . . . . The hidden guide lets no one enjoy great achievement without passing the persistence test. Those who can't take it simply do not make the grade.

There is one quality which one must possess to win and that is: definiteness of purpose, the knowledge of what one wants, and a burning desire to possess it.

Money is shy and elusive. It must be wooed and won by methods not unlike those used by a determined lover, in pursuit of the girl of his choice.

Time is the friend of the person who trains his mind to follow positive thought-habits and the enemy of the person who drifts into negative thought-habits.

Men and women who come to the closing chapter of life disappointed because they did not attain the goal which they had set their hearts upon achieving, they teach you what not to do.

Success comes to those who become success conscious.

Happiness is found in doing—not merely in possessing.

Your ship will not come in unless you have first sent it out.

An educated man is one who has learned how to get what he wants without violating the rights of others.

Happiness may be had only by helping others to find it.
Only those who have the habit of going the second mile ever find the end of the rainbow.

Control your own mind and you may never be controlled by the mind of another.

The ladder of success is never crowded at the top.

If you have no major purpose, you are drifting toward certain failure.

Great achievement is born of struggle.

Nothing great was ever achieved without a positive mental attitude.

The successful man keeps his mind fixed on that which he wants—not that which he doesn't want.

The end of the rainbow is reached only at the end of the second mile.

Whatever you think today becomes what you are tomorrow.

You can't control other men's acts, but you can control your mental reaction to their acts and that is what counts most to you.

If you must speak ill of another, do not speak it—write it in the sand near the water's edge.

If your mind can make you sick—and it can—remember it also can make you well.

It is a sure thing that you'll not finish if you don't start.

It is better to imitate a successful man than to envy him.

The imagination is the workshop of the soul wherein a man's destiny is fashioned.

Self-discipline is the first rule of all successful leadership.

A man without a definite major purpose is as helpless as a ship without a compass.

Remember that the quality of the service you render plus the quantity, plus the mental attitude in which you render it, determines the sort of job you hold and the pay you receive.

Remember that every defect and every disappointment and every adversity carries the seed of an equivalent benefit.

The most successful men are those who serve the greatest number of people.

If you wish a job done promptly and well, get a busy man to do it. The idle man knows too may substitutes and short cuts.

Opportunity has a way of getting near the man with a positive mental attitude.

Every thought a man releases becomes a permanent part of his character.

Anyone can quit when the going is hard, but a thoroughbred never quits until he wins.

No man can get to the top without carrying others along with him.

Drifting, without aim or purpose is the first of 30 major causes of failure

Trying to get without first giving is as fruitless as trying to reap without having sown.

NOTES

_____

_____

_____

_____

_____

_____

_____

_____

_____

_____

_____

_____

_____

_____

NOTES

NOTES